the HERO INSIDE YOU

the HERO INSIDE YOU

A 90 Day Journey to
PURPOSE, POWER *and the* PERSON
You were Meant to Be

TONY EDGELL

NEW YORK

the HERO INSIDE YOU
A 90 Day Journey to PURPOSE, POWER *and the* PERSON *You were Meant to Be*

Published in New York, New York, by Morgan James Publishing. Morgan James and The Entrepreneurial Publisher are trademarks of Morgan James, LLC. www.MorganJamesPublishing.com

The Morgan James Speakers Group can bring authors to your live event. For more information or to book an event visit The Morgan James Speakers Group at www.TheMorganJamesSpeakersGroup.com.

Visit TonyEdgell.com to receive 5 free videos to find purpose, power, and the Hero you were meant to be.

A FREE eBook edition is available with the purchase of this print book

CLEARLY PRINT YOUR NAME IN THE BOX ABOVE

Instructions to claim your free eBook edition:
1. Download the BitLit app for Android or iOS
2. Write your name in UPPER CASE in the box
3. Use the BitLit app to submit a photo
4. Download your eBook to any device

ISBN 978-1-63047-059-3 paperback
ISBN 978-1-63047-060-9 eBook
ISBN 978-1-63047-061-6 hardcover
Library of Congress Control Number: 2013957729

Cover Design by:
Rachel Lopez
www.r2cdesign.com

Interior Design by:
Bonnie Bushman
bonnie@caboodlegraphics.com

In an effort to support local communities, raise awareness and funds, Morgan James Publishing donates a percentage of all book sales for the life of each book to Habitat for Humanity Peninsula and Greater Williamsburg.

Get involved today, visit
www.MorganJamesBuilds.com.

Habitat for Humanity
Peninsula and Greater Williamsburg
Building Partner

Dedicated to my beautiful wife, Gail—thank you for travelling the Hero's Journey with me. To two of my greatest teachers Izzy and Bubba—always stay true to who you really are. To my Mum, who left us too early—may your loving, passionate and fun spirit shine through in me. Patricia and Maria—thank you for turning my words into sentences; God Bless Hero editors! Thank you to everyone I have come across on my Journey—you have been my real teachers.

CONTENTS

FOREWORD

It used to really frustrate me when I heard speakers, either on TV or stage, talk about finding and doing what our purpose is in life and loving what you do. The people who talked about this always made it seem so easy; like the next day I was going to wake up and realize, OH that's my purpose! They always had the same questions; like, "What do you love to do? "What are your hobbies? My wife and I were at a seminar, and one of the speakers was selling a program that helped you build websites and he said it was simple to find what the site should be on— just build it on your hobby, passion or purpose. My wife and I discussed purchasing the program and what I would have on my website. The only thing either one of us could come up with was a website on micro beers. So my purpose in life was to drink beer and evaluate micro beers, OK. This idea did not resonate with me, so I didn't do it.

I really wanted to know my purpose and wake up every morning excited for what I was destined in my heart to do, but I wasn't finding it, and I didn't know how to find it. I finally found it, and yes it's true—we do have a burning desire, a gift we want to share with the world. In this book, you will learn how to find your purpose, your heart's desire that fuels your passion, inspiration and excitement for life. I have taken a long and challenging journey to find this path to purpose. Now I am able to serve you. When you find and act on this gift, your life will transform and you will never be the same again.

I have found my gift! It's to show you how to find your heart's desires and purpose, and how to inspire and empower you to live your dreams. The more people that find this gift, the more beauty, passion, love, joy, peace and inspiration there will be in the world. My life is dedicated to you being a Hero and living the life you were meant to live. You know deep down inside there's something more out of life and you're entitled to have it. I believe in you. I believe in your dreams. You'll see in this book I love quotes. I'll end this foreword with quotes that are the purpose for the book and for my life.

I am here to serve. I am here to inspire. I am here to love. I am here to live my truth.

—**Deepak Chopra**

Your gifts are not about you
Leadership is not about you
Your purpose is not about you
A life of significance is about serving those who need your
    gifts, your leadership your purpose.

—**Kevin Hall**

To be creative means to be in love with life. You can be creative only if you love life enough that you want to enhance its beauty, you want to bring a little more music to it, a little more poetry to it, a little more dance to it.

—**Osho**

I love life and I am enhancing its beauty, music, poetry and adding a little more dance to it. To the Hero inside of you!

—**Tony Edgell**

Go to TonyEdgell.com/book-videos and watch foreword video.

Chapter 1

THE HERO
INSIDE OF YOU!!!

The meaning of life is to find your gift; the purpose of life is to give it away.

—**Joy Golliver**

I've come to believe that each of us has a personal calling that's as unique as a fingerprint - and that the best way to succeed is to discover what you love and then find a way to offer it to others in the form of service, working hard, and also allowing the energy of the universe to lead you.

—**Oprah Winfrey**

You are not the momentary whim of a careless creator experimenting in the laboratory of life. . . You were made with a purpose.

—Og Mandino

The only way to do great work is to love what you do. If you haven't found it yet, keep looking. Don't settle. As with all matters of the heart, you'll know when you find it.

—Steve Jobs

The universe has your back when you're living your soul's purpose.

—TUT... A Note from the Universe

The two most important days in your life are the day you are born, and the day you find out why.

—Mark Twain

I know we were put on earth to be joyous, feel good and have fun. I believe a lot of people have forgotten this, because they seem so unhappy with life and with themselves. The problem that I realized in myself, as well as in others, is that we chase happiness with what we think will make us happy. We are chasing the things that society has taught us to think are important. Going after the bigger house, a new car, the high paying job, what other people think of us, prestige and power. And when we get them, we want more. What I've experienced in my journey through life is that some of these things are nice to have, but they don't bring joy and inner peace. The life of a Hero is one where we are joyous for no specific reason, we feel inspired and alive, and we're in love with life. The way to experience this type of joy does not come from outside influences. You will realize this type of joy when you find the Hero Inside of You.

We are all born with the gift of a Hero inside of us. We know if we are living the life of a Hero through feelings—when we feel great, we are aligned with the Hero, life and purpose. Do you feel awesome? When you wake in the morning are you excited for another day? Are you filled with joy? Are you at peace with yourself and the world? Do you love yourself? Love your life? If the answer is yes, congratulations; keep doing what you're doing and close this book. You don't need to read any further, unless you would like to, of course. If the answer is no, congratulations and read on. That's the Hero inside of you letting you know that it desires to experience something different and more out of life.

My definition of a Hero is someone that is doing what they are called to do and love sharing their gift with the world. We recognize the Hero as being inspirational and courageous because they are being true to their purpose and not listening to what society believes they should be doing. And through this inspiration, their service makes the world more beautiful. The Hero is rewarded, because they feel great and joyful, are in love with life and live a life of dreams.

My life has been based on what people and society said would make me happy. I've worked the last 25 years for a paycheck. In my previous job, I worked for a nuclear plant that was owned by a huge company that treated their employees very well and the pay was great. I worked with some amazing people and the work was interesting, but there was always something missing for me. I never gave 100%, because my heart was never in the work that I was doing. I never woke up excited about going to work, especially on Monday mornings. I never felt inspired at my job and 40 hours a week is a long time in your life to feel uninspired. I sold my soul for money.

After a long journey of soul-searching, with lots of books, personal development courses, working on building wealth, I have discovered my Hero. Now I live from my heart. I am excited that I get to do something that I love and share it with the world.

I know you're reading this book, because you want to know your Hero and experience something new in life. You want to experience your natural state of joy, bliss, passion, abundance and feel alive. This is the life you were meant to live. Everything we have experienced in the journey of life was for life's lessons to be a Hero and serve from these experiences. This book will guide you on how to live from your heart as a Hero. It's time to start feeling good! So let's embark on this journey together where you get to meet the Hero Inside of You.

Imagine that five years ago you won the biggest lottery in history and you have traveled the whole world, have all the material things you ever wanted and done everything fun you could think of. You still have a lot of money and time and you want to do something for the world. What would that gift be? This is a clue in finding your heart's desires. If you thought of something great, think of it daily with a smile and curiosity. If you could not think of anything don't worry about, it will come to you.

Habits of Heroes

Smile and have fun every single day. Heroes are always smiling and having fun.

The Heroes' **I am** statements. Please take a few minutes several times a day to say these.

1. I am living my dreams.
2. I am full of joy.
3. I am feeling good.

Go to TonyEdgell.com/book-videos and watch chapter 1 video.

Chapter 2

BORN TO BE ALIVE

Your visions will become clear only when you can look into your own heart. Who looks outside, dreams; who looks inside, awakes.

—C.G. Jung

You are not your mother, your father, your history, or your cultural influences. You are uniquely and originally you. Be bold and daring and fearless and unconventional. Be willing to use your voice in service to your soul. Go on. Rock that damn boat. The wave you create might just change the world!

—Cheryl Richardson

The privilege of a lifetime is to become who you truly are.
—C.G. Jung

Reexamine all that you have been told in school, or in church or in any book. Dismiss whatever insults your soul.
—Walt Whitman

What stops us from finding and living our passion, dreams and heart's desires? I believe the main reason is what we have been taught to think or our programming. What is programming and how does it disempower us from living our dreams?

The brain is amazing. We learned how to roll over, crawl, walk, talk, write, spell, ride a bike, drive—the list goes on forever. It's amazing how much the brain can learn and absorb when something interests us or we want to learn or succeed in a career. The brain is the greatest computer ever made; it's an amazing super computer. We feed it information, it processes that information and forms a decision based on how our brain was programmed. Programmed? How does our brain become programmed?

Our programming started the day we were born. When we were children growing up, our brains were sponges that absorbed every piece of information that we saw and heard, and that information created our programmed brain. Who we came into contact with while growing up has a lot to do with our programming; family, society and culture played a big part in are programming. Now, obviously our parents didn't sit down and program us like a computer, but they played a huge part in what information and beliefs we learned.

I live in Lancaster, Pennsylvania – where the Amish live and are very prevalent. The Amish live a very simple life based on their religion. They don't use any of the modern amenities of society like electricity, television or phones. They don't drive cars; their way of transportation is with a horse and buggy. The men wear black suits with a solid colored shirt, straw hats and have beards. The women wear solid color dresses with long sleeves and a full skirt, covered with a cape on the bodice and white caps.

The interesting part of this is how we get programmed based on our upbringing. If we had Amish parents, our programming would be Amish and we would be Amish. It isn't common for someone that is brought up in the Amish community to stop being Amish and do something different; they don't usually make significant changes to their lifestyle and their programming. We tend to stay true to our original programming—what we knew growing up.

I have looked at different cultures around the world and thought if my parents were from that part of the world, from that culture, I would be living the same life they are. Observe people and without being judgmental, see if you can figure out what type of programming they received when they were growing up. Would you have the same beliefs they do if you had grown up in their family and culture? Other people's programming is easy to recognize, but it is much harder to see our own.

If you really think about it in the simplest of terms, a computer and our brain work in similar ways. It's not quite that simple, but in the general sense, we put things into a computer through a keyboard and we get an answer on the screen based on the programming. The brain develops programs by absorbing and observing the information around us while we were growing up, and as adults we get answers to questions and what we want to do from that program.

There are many people in our lives that contribute to our software. Parents who love us and want the best for us, grandparents, family members, teachers, coaches, religious leaders, authority figures and pretty much anyone that has come into our lives at some point. We could have had parents and other people that were not very loving or concerned about us. How did that affect programming? Our sources of programming were also programmed by the above sources and whomever they came in contact with.

One of the biggest programmers of our brain is the TV. I can't imagine how many hours of television I've watched in my lifetime. How many hours of television do you think you've watched in your lifetime? How many cologne ads have we watched where a man attracts beautiful women because of the cologne he is wearing? How many hours of commercials have we watched that said if we took this drug, it would take care of our problems and we would feel good? How many different commercials have we seen about buying this celebrity-endorsed exercise equipment and we will be thin, beautiful and our friends will envy us. All of the shows and commercials we've watched over the years were a major influence in programming our brain.

Some of the programming that we received growing up will sound very familiar, go to school, get good grades, get a good job, follow the rules of society so you fit in, be successful, success is measured by what you do and how much you have, security, being accepted and liked by people is extremely important and fear of the unknown and failure. Does that sound familiar?

The computer and the human brain are very similar in how they make decisions. The computer makes decisions without feelings and so does the human brain. Feelings come from the heart and they are love, joy, peace, compassion, empathy, generosity, kindness and many other feelings you can name. When we listen to our heart and allow it to guide us, our lives are full of passion, zest, fun, inspiration and purpose. If we didn't have a heart, we would be walking around without feelings like robots.

The majority of the time our conditioned mind (programmed brain) overrides what the heart desires. Some of these things could be when we want to help someone, volunteer, do something adventurous and dangerous, live somewhere different, quit our jobs and do something we love, travel, or do something we have always dreamed of doing. There are all kinds of stories the conditioned mind will come up with to stop us.

There is a battle going on inside each of us between our heart and our conditioned mind. The brain usually wins, because we unconsciously make decisions from programming and conditioning from our past. Programming is in the subconscious mind so most of the decisions we make are unconscious, they are made automatically, without us being aware and conscious. When the heart wants to do something that will bring us joy, be who we are meant to be and true to ourselves, our programming overrides the heart, stops us from living our dreams and having what is truly our heart's desire.

In this book, you will learn how unconscious programming in our lives stops us from living the life we were meant to live. And you will learn how to be conscious and get closer to your heart.

Here is a short story of what I am trying to convey to you.

A student was seeking a wise man to answer the questions he had about life. The student looked high and low for the wisest man on earth. He was finally told of a wise man in India, so he decided to sell all of his belongings and make the journey. After many months of looking for this wise man, he finally came upon a fragile old man who would lead him to his teacher. When he finally arrived he was very excited. Now he would have the opportunity to ask his long awaited questions. As he entered the room, the wise man asked him why he had made this journey. The student began to tell him the story and then the wise man stopped him and asked him if he wanted a cup of tea. The student told the wise man, "Sure, but I didn't come here to drink tea!" The wise man kept pouring the tea into the cup as the student continued talking. Finally, as he looked down to take a drink, he saw that the teacup was overflowing and the wise man was still pouring. The student yelled, "Stop! You're spilling tea all over the place!" The wise man stopped and answered, "Yes, you see the cup is like you my son. You cannot take in any more truth if you are unwilling to empty your mind and beliefs in order to learn more."

We have picked up beliefs from our journey through life. In order to be a Hero we need to empty our brains of the unconscious beliefs that disempower us from living from the heart and being alive.

> *Intelligence is a natural phenomenon - just as breathing is, just as seeing is.*
>
> *Intelligence is the inner seeing; it is intuitive. It has nothing to do with intellect.*
>
> *Never confuse intellect with intelligence, they are polar opposites.*
>
> *Intellect is of the head; it is taught by others, it is imposed on you.*
>
> *You have to cultivate it. It is borrowed, it is something foreign, it is not inborn.*
>
> *But intelligence is inborn. It is your very being, your very nature.*
>
> —Osho

Habits of Heroes

What beliefs do you have that are not yours that you have picked up through your journey in life? Give yourself some quiet time to think about that question.

The Heroes' **I am** statements. Please take a few minutes several times a day to say these.

1. I am living from my heart.
2. I am grateful for the journey I took in life and for everyone that was in the journey.
3. I am feeling good.

Go to TonyEdgell.com/book-videos and watch chapter 2 video.

Chapter 3

COURAGEOUS HEART

There are two forces in every human, one of love and giving, another of fear and taking. Each day we get the chance to decide which voice we will listen to. Yes, there is a voice inside each one of us few are willing to discuss. Which voice will each of us heed today? Will courage be the victor?

—Erol Fox

Your time is limited; don't waste it living someone else's life. Don't be trapped by dogma, which is living the result of other people's thinking. Don't let the noise of other's opinion drowned your own inner voice. And most important, have the courage to follow your heart and intuition, they somehow already know what you truly want to become. Everything else is secondary.

—Steve Jobs

You may be 38 years old, as I happen to be. And one day, some great opportunity stands before you and calls you to stand up for some great principle, some great issue, some great cause. And you refuse to do it because you are afraid…. You refuse to do it because you want to live longer…. You're afraid that you will lose your job, or you are afraid that you will be criticized or that you will lose your popularity, or you're afraid that somebody will stab you, or shoot at you or bomb your house; so you refuse to take the stand. Well, you may go on and live until you are 90, but you're just as dead at 38 as you would be at 90. And the cessation of breathing in your life is but the belated announcement of an earlier death of the spirit.

—Martin Luther King, Jr.

I believe really courageous people are the ones who listen to their heart. Why? Because listening to your heart and throwing away years of programming and conditioning on what society has told us will make us happy can be very challenging. It is doing the complete opposite of what your friends, family and almost everyone else are doing. That's why they are called Heroes; because they take the road less travelled. I know that you can overcome the challenges of living from your heart and live a joyful life as a Hero.

I would like to share a courageous story of a woman who used her heart as a guide.

Sitting Down

On Thursday evening December 1, 1955, after a long day of work as a seamstress for a Montgomery, Alabama department store, Rosa Parks boards a city bus to go home.

Tired as she is, Mrs. Parks walks past the first few — mostly empty — rows of seats marked "Whites Only." It's against the law for an African American like her to sit in these seats. She finally settles for a spot in the middle of the bus. Black people are allowed to sit in this section as long as no white person is standing. Though Rosa Parks hates the segregation laws, and has been fighting for civil rights at the NAACP for more than 10 years, until today she has never been one to break rules.

The bus continues along its route. After several more stops the bus is full. The driver notices that all the seats in the "Whites Only" section are now taken, and that more white people have just climbed aboard. He orders the people in Mrs. Parks's row to move to the back of the bus, where there are no open seats. No one budges at first. But when the driver barks at the black passengers a second time, they all get up . . . except for Rosa Parks.

Rosa Parks has finally had enough of being treated as a second-class citizen. As an African American, she has put up with terrible treatment on city buses, as well as in stores, restaurants, movie theaters, and other places for years. She is tired of it. In fact, she remembers that twelve years earlier this very same bus driver made her get off the bus and enter through the rear door.

When the driver continues shouting at her to move, Rosa Parks decides that she is not going to take it anymore. She simply says no, and refuses to get up from her seat.

The angry bus driver puts on the emergency brake, gets out of his seat and marches over to Mrs. Parks. He demands that she move to the back of the bus. When she doesn't, he leaves the bus and returns with a policeman. Mrs. Parks is promptly arrested for violating segregation laws. (Source: Scholastic, teacher. scholastic.com/rosa/sittingdown.htm, How I Fought for Civil Rights. *Website*)

Think about how scary it was sitting in that bus with a white guy screaming at you telling you to get up. The world was completely different back then, white people were killing black people and she had no idea if they were going to kill or beat her. She probably had a fear of going to jail. Think how you would feel about going to jail for a month. How scary is that? And this is a black woman going to jail that is run by white men who hate blacks. Think of the other black people on the bus who were probably telling her to get up and not start any problems. Another way we could look at this is society telling us not to listen to our heart. I can picture her sitting on the bus and saying to herself I am powerful and repeating that over and over again. By refusing to move on the bus, she single-handedly changed history and started the civil rights movement. She did this in a very simple and peaceful way. What a courageous woman and Hero.

I was a bully going through high school and when I started going to bars, I found myself getting into fights at the bars. I was always trying to prove how tough I was. I was very close to my mother, but when my mother passed away I didn't cry. I still remember my sister and wife questioning me as to why I wasn't crying. The reason I didn't cry was because I thought showing your emotions was a weakness. I was afraid people would think I was weak and not tough. Why did I think like this? Why was I out to prove how tough I was? Where did I get this software that was in my conditioned mind?

I thought about all the TV programs I watched in my life and the stereotypical male image that is abundant. The image is of a male who is tough and macho, or another way of saying it, someone who never shows feelings from the heart. They love to and are good at fighting and they kill bad guys. And my conditioned mind was taking all this information in when I watched actors like John Wayne and Clint Eastwood.

A few years ago I went to a personal development summer camp. At this camp something happened that triggered my feelings and caused me to cry, no it wasn't crying, it was bawling and it lasted for an hour or more. I guess everything that was built up in me came pouring out and it felt great to release it. Thank God I learned men do cry no matter what my conditioned mind was programmed to think.

A Hero is courageous because they listen to their heart, not the fear of being uncomfortable and doing something different created by the conditioned mind. Although the Hero is courageous, they show compassion and kindness to mankind. Heroes are in harmony with humanity and the world.

A few years ago I experienced firsthand the battle between the conditioned mind and listening to the heart and being courageous. The Hero inside was telling me that after I talked to my father on the phone I should tell him that I loved him. However, my conditioned mind was fighting me big time on this. While I was thinking about doing this, I kept hearing the programming telling me over and over again, men don't tell men they love each other and I had a slight grudge with my father about some things that happened in the past. I fought this internal battle for a few weeks. The day came when I decided to do it. When I was talking to my Dad on the phone I became sick to my stomach, I was sweating badly and my brain kept telling me how stupid and unmanly this idea was. The conversation ended and we were saying our goodbyes, with my heart pounding through my chest I said, I love you dad. YES, I DID IT! My courageous heart overwrote the programming from the conditioned mind. I can't begin to tell you how proud I am and the joy I feel by saying these words. Looking back on this, it feels very strange to me that I used to feel that way. Because now all of our conversations end with both of us saying that we love each other. It's so easy to do and I love doing it.

When my father was nine years old his father left his mother and four brothers for his mother's best friend and the father took the youngest one in the family—his sister. Because of this, my father grew up extremely poor and living in horrible conditions. When I was a child, my father befriended his father and they developed a good relationship. I can still remember questioning my father as a child about how he could allow his father back into his life after leaving his family high and dry. Thanks Pop! After 46 years I can finally answer that question myself—you showed me what forgiveness looks like. You had no one to lead by example, but you have always been a great father. I'm honored to say that I love my dad. He is definitely a Hero of mine. It is extremely rewarding when you change your programming and conditioning.

What are **you** willing to stay seated on the bus for? Whatever it is, do it with love. A Hero does everything with love and peace.

Here are two of my favorite quotes from Rosa Parks.

I believe we are here on the planet Earth to live, grow up and do what we can to make this world a better place for all people to enjoy freedom.

I would like to be known as a person who is concerned about freedom and equality and justice and prosperity for all people.

Here is another story of a courageous Hero for your heart to enjoy and feel.

Life in a Jar- The Irene Sendler Story

The following article is written by the Milken Family Foundation (www.mff.org) and is reprinted with the Foundation's permission.

Four of Milken Educator Norm Conard's (KS '92) students discovered an unsung Heroine of the Holocaust and spread her story around the world.

In 1942, as Jews throughout Europe were being rounded up and transported en masse to Nazi concentration camps to face an unthinkable fate, one woman took courageous action and risked her own life to save thousands of others.

Her name was Irena Sendler. Though she herself was not Jewish, she feared for the lives of Jews around her, particularly the children. As head of the children's section in the Polish underground movement known as Zegota, she was unable to sit by and not do anything. So she went into the Warsaw Ghetto and persuaded Jewish parents and grandparents to place their children in her care, saying that they were certain to die in the Ghetto or in the Nazi death camps unless they could be spirited away to safety.

Smuggling the children past Nazi guards through a variety of means – hiding them in body bags or under loads of goods – Ms. Sendler took them into the homes of Polish families, where they were adopted and raised with false identities. Ms. Sendler made lists of these children and placed the lists in a jar that she buried in a garden, hoping she could someday dig up the jar, locate the children and inform them of their past.

From 1942 to 1943, Ms. Sendler managed to smuggle 400 children out of the Warsaw Ghetto before she was captured by the Nazis and severely punished for her actions. Even under extreme torture, she refused to reveal where the lists of the smuggled Jewish children were hidden. Eventually, a member of the Polish underground bribed a guard to release her, and she entered into hiding. Even then, she continued to work with Zegota to rescue another 2,100 children.

It's a remarkable story, and considering all the remarkable stories from the Holocaust that have surfaced over the past several years, it's hard to believe that this one went largely unnoticed. And it might have stayed that way, were it not for four high school students from Uniontown, Kansas.

Changing the World

It began as a class assignment from their teacher, Milken Educator Norm Conard (KS '92): create a year-long project for the National History Day Competition that would, among other things, extend the boundaries of the classroom to families in the community, contribute to the learning of history, and meet the classroom motto, "He who changes one person, changes the entire world."

As the four girls – Elizabeth Cambers, Megan Stewart, Sabrina Coons and Janice Underwood – began doing their research, they discovered an article in U.S. News and World Report about Ms. Sendler, and they were surprised by the number of children she had saved.

"I thought it might have been a typographical error," said Mr. Conard, "since I had not heard of this woman nor her story."

The girls wrote a play based on her life called "Life in a Jar," which they entered into the National History Day Competition and began performing in front of numerous community organizations. What happened next is a story in itself.

The play was extremely well-received every time it was performed. Though Uniontown is a small community with little ethnic diversity and no Jewish residents, the response to the play was so extraordinary that the town designated an "Irena Sendler Day."

Assuming that Ms. Sendler was no longer living, the four students began a search for her final resting place. They were surprised to learn that she was still alive, living in poverty in Warsaw, Poland. They contacted Ms. Sendler, telling her of their project and the response it was getting. She wrote back letters written in Polish, which were translated with the help of a Polish student at a local Kansas college.

"Your performance and work is continuing the effort I started over fifty years ago," wrote Ms. Sendler. "You are my dearly beloved girls."

The girls decided to raise money on behalf of Ms. Sendler and other rescuers. They began taking a jar to each performance to collect donations. They contacted an organization in New York City called the

Jewish Foundation for the Righteous, which helped the girls send the money they had raised to a Polish bank in Warsaw.

At the same time, they began receiving national attention for the story they had "rediscovered," appearing on C-SPAN, National Public Radio, CBS, and numerous newspaper articles. They were invited to perform their play in Washington, D.C. and before the Jewish Foundation for the Righteous in New York City. Mr. Conard was contacted for the book and film rights to his students' story.

A True Heroine

One day in January 2001, the girls performed their play before a large school district in Kansas City, about 100 miles from Uniontown. In the audience was John Shuchart, a Jewish educator and businessman who was so moved by the performance that he asked to have lunch with Mr. Conard and his students that day. Hearing that Ms. Sendler was still alive, Mr. Shuchart told the girls he would raise the money to send them to Warsaw to meet her in person and bring back her story. Because she is 91 and in poor health, he urged the girls to travel as soon as possible.

Mr. Shuchart raised the money in 24 hours, and on May 22, 2001, Mr. Conard, his wife, the four students and several of their parents traveled to Warsaw, Poland, where they met Ms. Sendler in person.

It was an emotional moment. When this 91 year-old woman pushed her walker across her apartment to greet them, what the four young girls saw was a Heroine of immense stature. But with the modesty one often finds in truly Heroic people, Ms. Sendler characterized herself and her life as merely ordinary.

The girls still perform their play in front of local churches, civic groups and clubs, with performances booked until the summer of 2002. They continue to conduct research on Ms. Sendler's story and correspond regularly with Ms. Sendler and the people she rescued.

They have established an e-mail address - isendler@ hotmail.com - which receives daily messages from across the nation. Three more students have joined the group to help with all the email and research. They have donated their correspondence with Ms. Sendler to various universities, historical societies, and to the Jewish Foundation for the Righteous in Chicago and New York City. A local college professor has been using their letters from Ms. Sendler in his World History class.

The story of Irena Sendler has had a profound effect not only on those who have heard the story, but on the storytellers as well. The girls regularly write on their homework papers notes such as, "I'm changing the world" and "Irena's story must be told."

"I've traveled with the girls to numerous performances and watched the great emotion that pours out of the audience during their presentation," said Mr. Conard. "They have literally taken our class motto – 'He who changes one person, changes the entire world.' – and brought it to life. (Source: The Turner Foundation, hmturnerfoundation.org, artjar page. *Website*)

Habits of Heroes

Start out small, and do something your heart wants to do, but the conditioned mind doesn't want to. Overwrite that program.

The Heroes' **I am** statements. Please take a few minutes several times a day to say these.

1. I am courageous.
2. I am powerful.
3. I am feeling good.

Go to TonyEdgell.com/book-videos and watch chapter 3 video.

Chapter 4

LIVE LIKE YOU
WERE DYING

---

*We cannot become what we need to be by remaining what
we are.*

—**Max DePree**

We all make choices; but in the end our choices make us.
—**Andrew Ryan** (Bioshock)

*Everybody talks about wanting to change things and help and
fix, but ultimately all you can do is fix yourself. And that's a
lot. Because if you can fix yourself, it has a ripple effect.*

—**Rob Reiner**

It is not what we profess but what we practice that gives us integrity.

—**Unknown**

You must unlearn what you have learned.

—**Yoda**

My mission in life is not merely to survive, but to thrive; and to do so with some passion, some compassion, some humor, and some style.

—**Maya Angelou**

To attain knowledge, add things every day. To attain wisdom, remove things every day.

—**Lao Tzu**

As human beings, our greatness lies not so much in being able to remake the world as in being able to remake ourselves.

—**Mahatma Gandhi**

*W*OW! I've been on quite a journey for the last six years. I got involved in numerous courses that taught people how to become a millionaire and get rich. I invested money in stocks, real estate, multilevel marketing and an illegal pyramid scheme with the hopes of becoming rich. (No, I didn't know it was illegal until the government shut it down.) I invested in a business in California that turned out to be fraudulent and

I, along with many other people, lost money and the owner went to jail. You name it, I was involved in it. When I left these courses, I remember feeling very confused and bad about myself because I was questioning what I was doing wrong. I kept thinking one day I'd be rich and then I'd have what they're talking about.

While I was chasing riches, I noticed that I was starting to rot inside. I was starting to become hard inside, I wasn't as easygoing, I was less loving and family was less important to me. I was very judgmental of others. What was wrong with them not trying to get rich? They can't be happy living life that way. My ego became so big; I'm surprised my head didn't explode. The bottom line, I didn't like who was looking back at me in the mirror anymore, I didn't like who I had become.

There is nothing more painful than being on a journey that your Hero and heart don't want to be on. I've been on that journey my whole life. I've worked jobs for the money not because I loved them or was passionate. I've chased the money for many years because my conditioned mind had been programmed to believe that money makes you happy. I thought that in the future I would be happy when I had all the things that the riches could buy. My whole life changed when I got in touch with the Hero inside and started listening to my heart. I'm extremely grateful that this happened because I'm loving life and the world didn't change, I changed.

There was a time when we didn't know how to walk, talk, ride a bike, read, spell or do math, but we learned how to do each of these things. In all of these examples, it wasn't the world that changed; we changed.

It's difficult to change and admit that how we are currently experiencing our life isn't the way we want to move forward. Why is that so difficult? The conditioned mind hates to be wrong and the choices we make are unconscious from the conditioned mind. Empowerment comes from being curious and aware instead of knowing and unaware. Once again, the world doesn't change, we change. You and your life will be rewarded by choosing to experience the life of a Hero and living from your heart.

A Hero does not count how many years until retirement, how long until vacation and how many hours until the end of the workday. A Hero is in love with life and lives every day as if it were their last.

The lyrics to Live Like You Were Dying by Tim McGraw had been written below. Due to copyright laws, I was unable to keep the words to the song in the book. Please do a search for the lyrics to Live Like You Were Dying by Tim McGraw and read them as part of the journey to be a Hero.

Habits of Heroes

Live every day like it is your last.

The Heroes' **I am** statements. Please take a few minutes several times a day to say these.

1. I am thriving and passionate about my life.
2. I am loving life.
3. I am feeling good.

Go to TonyEdgell.com/book-videos and watch chapter 4 video.

Chapter 5

WOULD YOU RATHER
BE HAPPY OR BE RIGHT?

The purpose of our lives is to be happy.

—Dalai Lama

Human beings are perhaps never more frightening than when they are convinced beyond doubt that they are right.

—Laurens van der Post

Be miserable. Or motivate yourself. Whatever has to be done, it's always your choice.

—Wayne Dyer

Many persons have a wrong idea of what constitutes true happiness. It is not attained through self-gratification but through fidelity to a worthy purpose.

—Helen Keller

THE KEY TO A HAPPY LIFE ... isn't to manipulate the conditions around me so I can feel better, the key is to change the "meaning" I give it and feel happy no matter what happens.

—Elizabeth Richardson

Joy is not in things, it is in us.

—Charles Wagner

Would you rather be happy or right? Of course everyone would rather be happy than right. Believe it or not, we would rather stay true to our beliefs and be unhappy than to try correcting our programming and be happy. We'd rather hold on to beliefs than change the programming we have become accustomed to and not be wrong. The best example that I can share with you is the fighting of the Palestinians and the Jews over land for a long time. Both sides believe they are right, so they won't change the programming in their mind, they would rather be right and continue to kill and be killed. They pass this mind conditioning (programming) on to their children. They never question if they would rather be happy or right because they have been programmed to believe that being right is more important.

Where did we develop this programming and why is it so important to be right? If you think back to when we were in school, it was very important to get the answers right all the time. Whether it was on a test or being asked questions in class, the main goal was to get a perfect score each time. Nobody wanted to be wrong and look like they were stupid. The worst thing you could do was to get too many questions wrong. You would either get a failing grade or you would fail the class, depending on how many tests you failed. Remember when you would have to tell your parents that you flunked a test or out of a class? I don't know about you, but there were no excuses with my parents when I failed. I would get into a lot of trouble, be grounded or have the things I loved taken away from me. That's how our minds learned that being wrong wasn't a good thing. There have been other influences in our lives that have helped condition our minds to be right.

I would like for you to do an exercise for me. I'll call it the 24-hour bitch. I would like you to bitch about everything that you don't like and that bothers you for the next 24 hours. Here are a few ideas that can help get you started: the president, Republicans, Democrats, Jews, Protestants, Catholics, poor people, people on welfare, rich people, taxes, the price of everything, money, your job, coworkers, sports, your sports team, weather, gas, prices, war, TV shows, food, parents, spouse, family and other people. Go ahead—I'm sure that you will think of many more that are on a more personal level. Let them flow for 24 hours. You can write emails, post it on Facebook and let your friends know how you're feeling. I might even start a bitching holiday. When you have completed your 24 hours, check in with yourself to see how you felt during that 24-hour period? Did you feel happy and good? Did the problems you were bitching about get resolved? I'll answer the last question, NO; none of the problems were resolved by bitching. You can't get angry and upset enough to make the world a better place. Go ahead and try it. Think of something that really upsets you for 10 minutes; did the problem go away? How did you feel? Did you make the world a better place? So it's very obvious that getting upset only makes you feel worse, it doesn't solve anything. Feeling bad is the opposite direction we need to be moving toward to be a Hero.

A Hero chooses curiosity over knowing. They don't argue or justify their position because being right isn't important to a Hero. A Hero always picks kindness. As Wayne Dyer says, "would you rather be right or kind, always pick being kind". This was a lesson I had to learn the hard way. A Hero knows the only change they can make to better the world is to better themselves. As Gandhi said, "Be the change you want to see in the world".

To live our dreams, we must feel good and that takes being conscious and aware of how we feel. Do the things that I'm hearing, seeing and thinking make me feel good? Picture yourself when you've had a bad day and you're in a bad mood. What is running through your mind? Are you having negative or inspiring thoughts? I know when I'm in an unhappy place, my thoughts are not empowering. A Hero understands that feeling good and being happy has nothing to do with what's going on in the world, it has everything to do with who they are as a person.

The better we feel, the closer we are to being a Hero. Even if the conditioned mind doesn't agree with this, we must feel good to be able to find and realize our dreams. Be aware of how the following things make you feel. Do people around you empower you or tear you down? How do the conversations that friends have make you feel? How does the information on talk radio and TV make you feel? How does listening to or reading the news make you feel? How does violence make you feel deep down inside?

Life is all about choices. So, we can choose to believe what the old programming is telling us, what I'm feeding my mind has nothing to do with how I'm feeling. Or we can overwrite that programming and live our dreams. Will you do things you are conditioned to do or will you listen to your heart? Do you want to be right or be happy?

Before I started writing this chapter, my wife and I were having a conversation, and I made a comment about something I thought she should think about doing. She didn't like the idea of me telling her what was best for her so she got a little upset with me. We both walked away from the conversation feeling badly. I went down to my office to write this chapter and my pencil wouldn't move. I continued trying to write for another 20 minutes and I even tried to take a nap thinking that fatigue could be the problem. I finally went to her and apologized and told her that I loved her. I went to my office to write and within five minutes my pencil started moving and it never stopped. How you feel has everything to do with being a Hero.

Today I Will Make a Difference

Today I will make a difference. I will begin by controlling my thoughts. A person is the product of their thoughts.

I want to be happy and hopeful. Therefore, I will have thoughts that are happy and hopeful. I refuse to be victimized by my circumstances. I will not let petty inconveniences such as stoplights, long lines or traffic jams be my master. I will avoid negativity and gossip. Optimism will be my companion and victory will be my hallmark. Today I will make a difference.

I will be grateful for the next 24 hours that are before me. Time is a precious commodity. I refuse to allow what little time I have to be contaminated by self-pity, anxiety, or boredom. I will face this day with the joy of a child and the courage of a giant. I will drink each minute as though it is my last. When tomorrow comes, today will be gone forever. While it is here, I will use it for loving and giving. Today I will make a difference.

I will not let past failures haunt me. Even though my life is scarred with mistakes, I refuse to rummage through my trash heap of failures. I will admit them. I will correct them. I will press on victoriously. No failure is fatal. It's OK to stumble...I will get up. It's OK to fail...I will rise again. Today I will make a difference.

I will spend time with those I love; my spouse, my children, my family. A man can own the world but be poor for the lack of love. A man can own nothing and yet be wealthy in relationships. Today I will spend at least five minutes with the significant people in my world. Five quality minutes of talking, or hugging or thanking or listening. Five undiluted minutes with my mate, children, and friends.

Today I will make a difference. (*On The Anvil*, Max Lucado)

What do you choose today?

What do you choose to feed your conditioned mind?

Do you choose to listen to the Hero inside of you or the conditioned mind telling you that you're crazy? If you choose the Hero, you will be crazy happy.

> *What prices do we pay for our need to be right? What prices do our families and loved ones pay for our need to be right?*
>
> —**Daniel Gutierrez**

Habits of Heroes

Be aware of what things you are letting into your mind and how they are making you feel.

The Heroes' **I am** statements. Please take a few minutes several times a day to say these.

1. I am curious.
2. I am happy because I choose happiness.
3. I am feeling good.

Go to TonyEdgell.com/book-videos and watch chapter 5 video.

Chapter 6

COMPETITION OR
COOPERATION

Because you are unique, you are only truly in competition with others when you are not being true to yourself. The moment you are your true self, there will feel as if there is no true competition and you will shine.

—Dr. John Demartini

It is literally true that you can succeed best and quickest by helping others to succeed.

—Napoleon Hill

If you want to be incrementally better: Be competitive. If you want to be exponentially better: Be cooperative.

—**Unknown**

The only thing that will redeem mankind is cooperation.
—**Bertrand Russell**

If you want others to be happy, practice compassion. If you want to be happy, practice compassion.

—**Dalai Lama**

During the summer months, my family would have picnics, and we all love to play kick ball. A few years ago, we were having the traditional kickball game and my nine year-old niece, Izzy, was pitching for my team. We were getting killed, and the other team's family members were talking smack. The longer we played, the more they'd score, and the more they scored, the madder I got. After one of the innings ended, we were leaving the field and I told Izzy that she wasn't going to pitch anymore. I said that I was going to pitch, and she responded by saying that she was going to pitch, which upset me even more. I said, "we'll see about that". When they got their third out, and my team was heading back to the outfield, Izzy quickly ran to the pitcher's mound, grabbed the ball and said she was going to pitch. Of course I said, "No, I'm pitching; give me the ball". She said, "No!" and held on to the ball. (Looking back on this my niece was probably thinking I can't believe my uncle's acting like this; I'm just trying to have fun.) I grabbed the ball out of her arms, and when the ball pulled out it hit her in the lip. She ran off crying and hurt with a bloody lip.

Just picture the scene, it's about 50% adults and 50% children so I'm playing with a bunch of children for fun, and I've just taken all the fun out of the game! After coming to my senses, I felt horrible. How could I act like such a monster, and how could winning a stupid kick ball game mean so much to me? I couldn't apologize enough to Izzy, and it bothered me for weeks. How could I be so competitive and act so badly? This was a very hard lesson for me to learn in life.

In my younger years, I have always loved and played sports and always loved to win. I used to watch a lot of sports on TV and always got upset if my team lost. Why was I so competitive? The answer is the conditioned mind loves competition. I'm not saying everyone is as competitive as I used to be in sports, but the conditioned mind is very competitive when it comes to people and humanity.

Once again, all you have to do is look back at your childhood and what you saw growing up. Grab the remote control for the TV and flip through the channels. All you'll see is competition and more competition; anything from a hot dog eating contest to playing cards and anything in between. Competition even goes as far as high schools having homecoming queens. I have to wonder how all the other girls in the same school and grade feel knowing they didn't win. Is that telling the other girls they're not as pretty, don't have as good of a personality or that they aren't as good as the winner?

What society really loves and honors are winners. The conditioned mind has observed that there is nothing more important than winning. Do whatever it takes for you to win, take drugs, cheat or whatever it takes, but for God's sake don't lose. There have been death threats against professional athletes who have made a mistake in a big game. Death threats for making a mistake—damn! The conditioned mind love to win. We have been a part of or heard the conversations when someone was complaining about their sports team. They would be saying why they didn't do this or that, and I wish they'd fire or get rid of that player or coach. It's rare after someone's team loses that you hear them say their team did great and gave 100%. Whatever it takes to win! The quote we have grown up with and society loves is, winning isn't everything, it's the only thing, from Vince Lombardi. The conditioned mind has learned by observing lots of competitions, how to be very competitive and that winning is everything.

I'm not saying that we should get rid of sports; I'm making you aware that the conditioned mind has been programmed to be very competitive. It competes for money, food, land, oil, power, ribbons, cars, trophies and the biggest and best homes. We always feel like we're in a competition, but the only one we're competing against is ourselves and our programming.

What does the Hero want? It wants to cooperate with mankind, not compete against them. It always has compassion for people and a deep understanding for everyone's journey in life and cares enough to take care of others. (The Hero cares deeply.) Imagine if everyone thought like this, there would be world peace and no one dying from starvation.

You get world peace through inner peace. If you've got a world of people who have inner peace, then you have a peaceful world.

—**Wayne Dyer**

The Hero is no longer competing with humanity, it's cooperating with it. It understands that we're all the same flesh and blood no matter what country you live in, what color your skin is or what economic conditions we live in. It knows how fast someone does something and the score on the scoreboard is for entertainment. It understands the greatest reward in life is to serve, give and share with mankind.

What do you choose? Do you choose the conditioned mind that has been programmed to compete or what your heart wants, cooperation? Allow yourself to feel what your heart wants.

Sports doesn't build character, it reveals it.

Ike's story is about much more than one touchdown run.

SNOHOMISH — Three years ago, Kay and Steve Ditzenberger were concerned that their son Ike was losing his brightness.

He was in a slump. His smile was fading. His energy was low. He seemed content to sit in the back of the auditorium for assemblies, ride in the back of the bus to school.

He was becoming disengaged, more accepting of the mistaken idea that, because he was born with Down syndrome, he was limited.

So holding hands as they walked into Coach Mark Perry's classroom, Kay, Steve and Ike came to the Snohomish High School football coach and asked if he would allow Ike to play for the Panthers.

Ike's brother Josh had played high-school football at Woodinville and collegiately at Dixie State and Central Washington. Ike wanted to be like Josh.

Perry poked roly-poly Ike in the stomach, told him he had to lose a little weight, then said, "You're going to be a part of this football team for the next four years."

"From that point on, we've kind of been buddies," Perry said.

Perry's classroom at Snohomish is across the hall from the classroom for the special-needs students. He sees them every day. He talks with them, teases them, hugs them, high-fives them and loves them.

Almost intuitively he understood how football could help Ike Ditzenberger, and just as important, how Ike's presence could help his team.

"Ike has a way of making people's days around here with just a smile," Perry said. "Everybody in the school knows him. He's a challenge sometimes. He's a handful sometimes, but he's contagious in his actions. Ike is always full of energy.

"Sometimes maybe I can be too serious and he can bring me right back, reminding me that we're supposed to be having fun. He can bring things down to the important things in life."

It has been a difficult season for Snohomish, which won its first game after five consecutive defeats, 21-17 on a Friday night over Marysville-Pilchuck. Ike has helped lend perspective to the season. "As coaches, we're defined by ours wins and losses," Perry said. "It's a big part of the picture. We'd love to be undefeated, but I think my children are learning more than just Xs and Os and football. And if they learn to treat another human being with humanity and compassion, we're all going to be better off."

Perry, who also coaches Ike on the wrestling team, designed a couple of plays for Ditzenberger.

The Ike Special is a running play that sends Ditzenberger up the middle. And the Ike Special is a kind of a swing pass.

With 10 seconds left in a recent home game, Snohomish was losing to rival Lake Stevens 35-0. The thought of shutting out Snohomish was sweet for the Vikings.

Perry called a timeout and came on the field to tell the Lake Stevens players he was going to run the Ike Special. He told the Vikings' defensive coordinator, Joe Cronin, about the play.

"I don't want you guys to lose your shutout," Perry told the players. "Preserve your shutout. You've earned it. But I'd like you to let Ike run around for 10 or 20 yards before you tackle him."

A year earlier, when Ike was on the Snohomish junior varsity team, the Panthers ran the same play against Lake Stevens and Ditzenberger scored. Many of those same Lake Stevens players were on the field for the final minutes of this game.

"We get it, coach," a Vikings player said, giving Perry a thumbs-up before the snap.

The subsequent play turned into something much more than a touchdown run. It was an all-encompassing act of human tenderness that, because of a YouTube video, was witnessed around the world.

"I've told my players I've learned more from them than they learned from me on that play," Lake Stevens coach Tom Tri said. "They were levelheaded enough to use their common sense. They weren't directed to do anything other than let Ike run for a while. But they took that literally and allowed Ike to score a touchdown.

"In hindsight, that was clearly the right thing to do. We didn't want to give up a shutout. This was one of our biggest rivals and we had a chance to shut them out on their home turf. But our players didn't even want to think about that. Their only thought was, 'Let's do the right thing.'"

Although the play is designed to go up the middle, Ike swung to the left. He actually ran out of bounds, but Perry urged him back into the field.

Ike cut right and toward the end zone as his teammates threw faux blocks and the Lake Stevens players dived and jumped and swung-and-missed at tackle attempts. Ike rode the wave of cheers from his teammates and the student body for a 51-yard touchdown.

"The Lake Stevens players, they made this happen for a special kid named Ike," Perry said. "They gave us a moment that none of us will ever forget."

Junior running back Jordan Holland, a regular who wasn't in the game, ran stride-for-stride with Ike, down the sideline, making sure Ike stayed focused and in bounds.

"I heard screaming in my ears," said Ike, a 17-year-old, 5-foot-6, 160-pound junior.

This should have been a difficult night for Snohomish, a bitter defeat in a disappointing season.

But the understanding of the Lake Stevens players and the unquenchable brightness of Ike made this moment and this game as unforgettable as a Super Bowl.

They celebrated the score as if it were the game-winner.

Holland was the first player to greet Ike after the touchdown. He lifted Ditzenberger in the air. Players mobbed Ike and encouraged him to do a touchdown dance.

He accommodated them. It was a moment of unambiguous joy.

"I was sprinting down the sideline and when I got to Ike I picked him up and he's pretty heavy and I almost hurt my back," Holland said. "We'll always remember that play. Every time we look at the picture we'll think of Ike. We'll remember all the things we've done with him. All the funny moments."

Ike ran back to the sideline and raised his helmet, acknowledging the cheers of the crowd.

"The smile on his face was priceless," said Perry, who has been in coaching for 28 years. "He knew he had done something special. He knew he'd scored a touchdown. He knew he'd succeeded in what he was trying to do."

While Ike was running, Tony Soper from Lake Stevens was recording every remarkable yard. The video he posted on YouTube went viral, getting more than a million views. The Ike Special took on a life of its own.

Both Perry and Tri got emails and letters from around the world, thanking them for their profound acts of sportsmanship.

"This thing's blossomed into something huge through no purpose or intent of ours," Perry said. "We gave one opportunity to one kid for one rep and in no way do you ever think that it would balloon into what it has. Ike's special to us no matter what happened."

But Ike's story is about much more than this one football play.

It is a reminder of the infinite capacity of the human heart. It is about Mark Perry's compassion. It is about the ability of the young players from Lake Stevens to understand the importance of the moment and act selflessly when it would have been so easy to be selfish.

It is about the Snohomish team's unconditional love of their teammate and about Ike's parents' love for their child.

"We've seen Ike brighten," Kay Ditzenberger said. "He no longer sits in the back at the assembly. He's right there in the front row. Football has elevated his self-opinion. He doesn't feel different. He doesn't perceive his handicap. They've given him the gift of normalcy.

"They (Snohomish players) set aside the handicap and saw the person first. They recognize the handicap secondly and they accommodate and adapt to that."

Last week, the Ditzenbergers went to Lake Stevens' practice.

"You could see in their faces that they were really proud of what they'd done," Kay said.

She spoke to the players.

"Thank you for your sacrifice, because in sacrifice is great power," she told them. "You unleashed something very powerful on the field two weeks ago that the world needed to see and hear. Your sacrifice touched the hearts of millions of people. We salute you Vikings."

She read a quote from the late UCLA basketball coach, John Wooden: "You can't live a perfect day without doing something for someone who will never be able to repay you."

At the end of the practice, Lake Stevens invited Ike to run their final play.

"I've learned from this that people can be true," Snohomish assistant coach Vince Ivelia said. "In a society that has a lot of the "me" attitude, this is an example of what we can do for others."

Ike's was a touchdown run like no other. It was a touchdown run that all of us should remember, a reminder of everything that is good about sports and about life. (Source: Steve Kelley, Seattle Times, seattletimes.nwsource.com/html/stevekelley/2013128361_kelley11.html, Ike's Story is About Much More Than One Touchdown Run. *Website*)

Habits of Heroes

Ask yourself, how can I give, share and serve humanity and the world.

The Heroes' **I am** statements. Please take a few minutes several times a day to say these.

1. I am cooperating with humanity and the world.
2. I am kind.
3. I feel good.

Go to TonyEdgell.com/book-videos and watch chapter 6 video.

Chapter 7

QUESTIONING ATTITUDE

Unthinking respect for authority is the greatest enemy of truth.

—Albert Einstein

Believe nothing, no matter where you read it, or who said it, no matter if I have said it, unless it agrees with your own reason and your own common sense.

—Buddha

I am the master of my fate: I am the captain of my soul.

—William Ernest Henley

I would rather have a mind opened by wonder than one closed by belief.

—**Gerry Spence**

A mind is like a parachute. It doesn't work if it is not open.
—**Frank Zappa**

Rather than looking at the unanswered questions, we must look at the unquestioned answers of our time.

—**Lynne Twist**

One of the greatest enemies of being a Hero and living from your heart is the ability to be open to a new way of thinking. If we go through life focused only on what we have been programmed to believe and being closed to everything else, we don't allow any room for growth. A very important part of becoming a Hero and being your true self is being open to new ideas and beliefs.

Why is this chapter so important? It is important to living the life you were meant to live. We've been programmed to believe that the way we think is the right way and only way, so it's very hard to be open to a new way of thinking. I'm not asking you to completely disregard everything you were programmed to think. I'm not telling you not to question things that you are unsure of either. Actually, quite the opposite—I'm asking you to question and think about all things. Be open to new ideas and knowledge.

Don't completely disregard things because it is unfamiliar to you and not from your programming.

For example, there was a time everyone thought the world was flat. Then people started saying that the world was round and most people were unable to believe this. They had been programmed to think that the world was flat. Years ago in America, people thought they owned someone simply because of the color of their skin. They had been taught and conditioned that their skin color was superior.

Adolf Hitler had an entire nation programmed to believe they should invade the world to rule it and they needed to kill all Jews. Not that long ago women weren't allowed to vote in the United States. Back in those days, everyone was programmed to think that men were superior to women. Not that long ago, black people were not allowed to vote, drink out of the same water fountain, go to the same schools or go the same church as white people. Nobody, including the leaders of the churches, found anything wrong with not allowing black people to attend church. Why? Everyone was listening to the programming from their conditioned mind and not their hearts.

What is the solution to our conditioned and closed mind? To have a questioning attitude and a mind that questions the status quo and society. To have a questioning attitude for everything you hear, see and read; rumors and facts help us to find our truth under all the layers of conditioning.

We all have a questioning attitude when it's something that's in our belief system or our conditioned mind. What I'm talking about is questioning what we believe and don't believe and why?

In today's society, we live in a time when questioning the status quo is looked down on and frowned upon. I've been through this experience several times in my life; I questioned something and didn't go along with the group's way of thinking. Someone would say, "oh, you're one of those people that doesn't trust the government" or "you think someone's out to get you". The pull from society is extremely strong, but the Hero inside of you is much more powerful.

I know while I was growing up, having a questioning attitude was not something that was encouraged, it was frowned upon. It wasn't like when you were in school, if you questioned something that the teacher said, that they admired your questioning attitude. No. If you had too many of those questions, you would be in the principal's office and your parents would be told that you were a troublemaker. This was just the beginning of learning how to fit in with society and be complacent. We learned at an early age that there is no reward for standing out and speaking our truth.

One day at the nuclear plant, they announced they would be giving free flu shots. Throughout the day, I watched about 99% of the people I work with get flu shots. I don't think many of them, if any, did research on flu shots and questioned them. I'm not saying that flu shots are good or bad, but I'm using this example to show you what complacency and not having a questioning attitude looks like. We can do research and question if we want to put those drugs in our body. Does a doctor or pharmaceutical company know what's better for me then I do?

Another day at work, I was having a conversation with a very intelligent and extremely religious coworker about the Iraq war and how many civilian casualties there were. He told me that civilian deaths are a part of war and that we have to kill the Muslims before they kill us because the Koran says all non-believers should be killed. I told him that I'd never read the Koran, but I didn't believe that's what it said. He kept insisting that's what it said and that he was right, I continued to doubt him. Then he took me to a coworker who was a "Koran expert" who told me the exact same thing the first guy told me. Later on I decided to do my own research on Google and found that what they were telling me was the complete opposite. I printed the information from various sites and left it on his desk. Once he read it, the only comment he had was that he thought one of the sites was owned by Muslims. He never talked about this subject again. Your programmed beliefs are very powerful, be aware of them.

I truly believe that if more people in the world did this, we would live in a completely different world. I would love to see politicians announce that they were going to invade another country and go to war, but have the majority of the country question if that was the best solution. Let's put it this way, it would be a huge step toward peace.

Another area that I notice a non-questioning attitude is between political parties. Again, it's not my job to say who's right or wrong, but from my perspective, people that are really committed to one party or another don't ever question their party or what it stands for. There's a lot of finger pointing at the other party and they believe that their party does no wrong. Most of these people would vote for anyone as long as they are wearing their Republican or Democrat team jersey. It's time to start questioning all leaders and ourselves as to why we believe so much in that particular political party. Where did the belief and programming come from that one political party has all the answer? Come on you can do it. Would you rather be right or happy?

I really want you to think about this. What Hitler did to the world and the Jews was completely legal in his country. Really think about that. How complacent were all the citizens of Germany? The complacent, non-questioning, conditioned mind can be very powerful, scary and a violent force. We can never allow something like this to happen again.

Think of some of the more recent Heroes. Rosa Park questioned the authority telling her where to sit on the bus. Martin Luther King, Jr. questioned why his skin color made him a second class citizen. Nelson Mandela spent 27 years in prison, because he didn't believe in what authorities were telling him. He later became the President and leader of South Africa, the same country that imprisoned him.

You are a powerful Hero; don't let anyone else do the thinking for you. Question everyone—doctors, political and religious leaders, teachers, television, anything you hear from someone else, the expert in their field, rumors, news, newspapers and the biggest one of all, yourself.

The easiest thing in the world is to be complacent and believe everything we hear. But a Hero is never complacent; they always use a questioning attitude. We can't allow anyone to tell us what is best for us. We are filled with wisdom; we know what's best for us. Only you know your truth and you will find it deep down in your heart.

Would you rather be a Hero or right?

Here is one last thought from Buddha that expresses the message of this chapter perfectly.

Do not believe in anything simply because you have heard it. Do not believe in anything simply because it is spoken and rumored by many. Do not believe in anything simply because it is found written in your religious books. Do not believe in anything merely on the authority of your teachers and elders. Do not believe in traditions, because they have been handed down for many generations. But after observation and analysis, when you find that anything agrees with reason and is conducive to the good and benefit of one and all, then accept it and live up to it.

—**Buddha**

Habits of Heroes

Question everything you read, hear and your own beliefs.

The Heroes' **I am** statements. Please take a few minutes several times a day to say these.

1. I am wisdom.
2. I am using a questioning attitude.
3. I am feeling good.

Go to TonyEdgell.com/book-videos and watch chapter 7 video.

Chapter 8

WHAT ARE YOU FOR?

Everything you are against weakens you. Everything you are for empowers you.

—Wayne Dyer

Never look down on anybody unless you're helping them up.

—Jesse Jackson

The highest form of human intelligence is to observe others without judgement.

—Jiddu Krishnamurti

No one truly knows what they will do in a certain situation until they are actually in it. It's very easy to judge someone else's actions by what you assume your own would be, if you were in their shoes. But we only know what we THINK we would do, not what we WOULD do.

—**Ashly Lorenzana**

Criticism of others is thus an oblique form of self-commendation. We think we make the picture hang straight on our wall by telling our neighbors that all his pictures are crooked.

—**Fulton J. Sheen**

Gossip is when you hear something you like about someone you don't.

—**Earl Wilson**

*I*sn't pointing your finger at someone and judging them the easiest thing in the world to do? The conditioned mind loves to talk and complain about other people; it's easy but it makes us feel bad. And we know how important feeling good is to being a Hero.

Go ahead and test this theory. Think of someone that upsets you or that you don't like and start saying negative things about them. How does that make you feel deep at your core? Criticizing people is what we have been programmed to do, so we are comfortable running the only program we know. If you are talking about other people, this is your Hero telling you that something is missing in your life.

I hear people saying bad things about people and I feel sorry for them because they must be hurting and not feeling well. I have observed people teasing and joking with others and there is nothing that's off limits; they talk about someone's family, someone's divorce, wife, people's appearance, etc., as long as they laugh after they say it, it's assumed it's a joke and accepted. I love to joke and have fun with people, but there is a difference between jokes that hurt people and have nothing to do with having fun. It's not fun or funny, it's hurtful.

On TV there are channels filled with people sitting around and judging other people. These people get paid huge amounts of money to do this. They are critical of people's actions and decisions and have all the answers to the way they think someone should have done something. There are also several 24-hour sports channels where some of the conversations are based on judging athletes, what they should've done versus what they did. We have observed this and it has helped program our conditioned mind.

My whole life changed when I started noticing what was right with people and the world, not what was wrong. Having the ability to see the good in people and the world is one of the greatest gifts I gave to myself. I used my heart as a guide because the heart only sees the good in everything. This totally transformed my life. Great quotes on this subject:

Step number one for changing the entire world, is falling in love with it as it already is. The same is true for changing yourself.

—TUT... A Note from the Universe

Seek not to change the world, but choose to change your mind about the world. What you see reflects your thinking. And your thinking but reflects your choice of what you want to see.

—A Course in Miracles

If you correct your mind, the rest of your life will fall into place.

—Lao Tzu

Heroes never point fingers at other people, place blame or talk about people. A Hero understands that words are very powerful and they can be used to empower someone or tear them down. They choose words that empower people. A Hero doesn't complain; they are always very grateful for everything in life.

Something I attempted to do in the past was make the U.S. government more accountable and make people aware of what was going on in the government. I had a website with videos and I talked about how much money the government was wasting, what we spent on wars and elections and there were homeless children in America. Or another way of saying it, I pointed my finger and placed blame. I never shared what I was for, only want I was against. While I was doing this I never checked in with my Hero to see how I was feeling. Thank God, after placing blame for some time, I eventually checked in with myself and noticed I didn't feel good doing this.

A Hero knows and talks about what they stand for, not what they're against. And this is what I'm for. I know everyone came to earth to be a Hero, to share and contribute a special gift to the world and when a person gives their gift to the world they will be filled with joy and abundance, be alive and in love with life, and the more people that share their gift, the more beautiful the world is.

What is something that really upsets you about the world and you wish were better? What would the world look like if it was the opposite of what upsets you? That is what you are for. What is something that happened to you in the past that you don't want anyone else to go through? These are clues for what the Hero inside of you wants to do. Be a Hero and know what you stand for and focus on that. Promote what you love instead of what you hate.

The Cookie Thief
by Valerie Cox

A woman was waiting at an airport one night,
With several long hours before her flight.
She hunted for a book in the airport shops.
Bought a bag of cookies and found a place to drop.

She was engrossed in her book but happened to see,
That the man sitting beside her, as bold as could be.
Grabbed a cookie or two from the bag in between,
Which she tried to ignore to avoid a scene.

So she munched the cookies and watched the clock,
As the gutsy cookie thief diminished her stock.
She was getting more irritated as the minutes ticked by,
Thinking, "If I wasn't so nice, I would blacken his eye."

With each cookie she took, he took one too,
When only one was left, she wondered what he would do.
With a smile on his face, and a nervous laugh,
He took the last cookie and broke it in half.

He offered her half, as he ate the other,
She snatched it from him and thought... oooh, brother.
This guy has some nerve and he's also rude,
Why he didn't even show any gratitude!
She had never known when she had been so galled,
And sighed with relief when her flight was called.
She gathered her belongings and headed to the gate,
Refusing to look back at the thieving ingrate.
She boarded the plane, and sank in her seat,
Then she sought her book, which was almost complete.
As she reached in her baggage, she gasped with surprise,
There was her bag of cookies, in front of her eyes.

If mine are here, she moaned in despair,
The others were his, and he tried to share.
Too late to apologize, she realized with grief,
That she was the rude one, the ingrate, the thief.

How many times in our lives,
have we absolutely known
that something was a certain way,
only to discover later that
what we believed to be true ... was not?

The conditioned mind judges and comes to conclusions; the heart loves to share.

Habits of Heroes

Do something kind every day for someone, but tell no one. Also be very kind to yourself every day.

The Heroes' **I am** statements. Please take a few minutes several times a day to say these.

1. I am empowering others with my words.
2. I am wonderful and the world is wonderful.
3. I am feeling good.

Go to TonyEdgell.com/book-videos and watch chapter 8 video.

Chapter 9

THE SECOND GREATEST LIE

When I chased after money, I never had enough. When I got my life on purpose and focused on giving of myself and everything that arrived into my life, then I was prosperous.

—Wayne Dyer

People are made to be loved and things are made to be used... The confusion in this world is that people are being used and things are being loved...

—Unknown

I can honestly say that I have never gone into any business purely to make money. If that is the sole motive, then I believe you are better off doing nothing.

—Richard Branson

To many people, success means making lots of money and having lots of things and a title that makes them feel proud. And there is nothing wrong with that, if that's what truly brings you joy. To me, true success means contributing something of significance to our Universe AND having a balanced life that I truly enjoy. The main purpose of money to me is that it provides me the freedom to do and have whatever I want, whenever I want. And I do enjoy luxury.

—Bela Patel

Often people attempt to live their lives backwards; they try to have more things, or more money in order to do more of what they want so they will be happier. The way it actually works is the reverse. You must first be who you really are, then do what you need to do in order to have what you want.

—Margaret Young

Throughout our life, the message we have been led to believe more than any other is that money and materialism will make us happy. Since we were young children, we have seen commercial after commercial of buy this car, wear this perfume, buy these clothes and jewelry, buy this big screen TV, a bigger house, a new car, run up your credit card, spend, spend, spend and you'll be happy, happy, happy. And our conditioned mind has been writing buy, buy, buy into its programming. The more we buy, the more the conditioned mind tells us to buy something else to make us happy. It's a never-ending cycle that our programming is running. We have been so conditioned to believe that buying makes us happy that people are willing to have lots of credit card debt to try to satisfy this programming. The conditioned mind has been programmed to believe the lie that having more things will bring us happiness. I'm not saying that there is anything wrong with having great things in life, but there is a huge difference between having them, enjoying them and chasing after them, believing they will bring happiness.

Okay, stop the presses and take a deep breath, close your eyes and ask yourself if you would rather be happy or right? I know this is a hard pill to swallow, because I used to chase money and riches thinking it would make me happy. Remember, you're holding this book in your hand for a reason. The reason is that you know deep inside that you're entitled to joy every day of your life. In order to feel the joy you will need to unlearn some things that you have been taught and were programmed to believe your whole life. Okay, now that you're relaxed, let's continue.

Think of all the rich people you know or have seen on TV. Do they all appear like they're joyful and feeling great? If money and things will make you happy then why aren't all rich people happy? Some of them actually seem miserable to me. How many celebrities who had all the money and fame that anyone could have in a lifetime died from drugs? If you have an excess of money, and money makes you happy why do you need drugs to make you feel good?

Imagine if you won $100 million in the lottery. I believe most people would be very happy when they won and were buying things for themselves and loved ones. But I believe there is a time after winning that you will go back to the same level of happiness that you were before you won the lottery. That will be the time you realize that material things will not bring you joy and peace. There have been studies done on people that have won the lottery and the majority of them were happier before they won the lottery.

The conditioned mind believes that what we do is who we are—electrician, construction worker, CEO, accountant, lawyer, truck driver, nurse, policeman, etc. We spend a lot of time, money and energy becoming the things society tells us will make us happy and comfortable. The Hero knows what we do for a living doesn't make us any more valuable. The Hero does what they are passionate about and what makes them come alive. Their joy and passion comes from giving a gift from their heart. They have it all—success, abundance, a good quality of life, freedom, bliss, health, joy and peace by sharing their gift with the world.

There is a huge amount of pressure from society to be successful according to society's standards. The conditioned mind is programmed to work ourselves to death just to prove that we were "successful and valuable". And what do most people sacrifice for that? Time with family and friends, health, joy, peace is what we sacrifice for that feeling of success. And we are left feeling like failures, because we think we should be doing more in order to be more valuable. When I was in the workforce, I witnessed this sad conditioning by some of my fellow coworkers.

Most people are so busy checking off their to-do list and busy doing, doing, doing, that their lives are passing them by. We have been programmed to be doers, but the Hero wants to experience being alive and living life by being. We are human beings not human doers. The Hero experiences being by going to the park, reading a book, spending time with loved ones, meeting and talking to a stranger, hobbies, slowing down, experiencing something it's never done, playing and having lots of fun and laughter and giving their gift to the world. On a typical day, observe the type of day you're having and others around you, is everyone doing or being? When you pass strangers on the street, are they celebrating life and giving you a huge smile and a hello, or are they listening to the conditioned mind and thinking about what they need to do next?

I'll give you an example of my life. I have rental properties, and one day I was going to fix up one of the units. While I was driving there, I found myself dreading doing this work and that's when the light bulb went on in my head. I thought to myself, you have no love for rental homes; you're only doing this for the money. That statement could not have been more accurate. I don't like and am not good at doing repairs, bookkeeping or tenant management, so why else would I own rentals? I believe there are people that love to do repairs and take care of tenants; this is their passion, and they should be rewarded financially. I also believe there are people who love to run businesses and the money is secondary to them; they do it because they love it.

I know when you find the Hero inside of you and your gift, you will have abundance. In addition, you wake up every day absolutely loving what you get to do. No more vacations; every day is vacation! The Hero knows success and abundance without chasing materialism. Three great quotes on success and abundance:

> *Abundance is the freedom to do what you want to do when you want to do it because you want to do it.*
>
> —**Daniel Gutierrez**

> *Success is doing what you want to do, when you want, where you want, with whom you want, as much as you want.*
>
> —**Anthony Robbins**

> *To laugh often and much; to win the respect of intelligent people and the affection of children; to earn the appreciation of honest critics and endure the betrayal of false friends; to appreciate beauty, to find the best in others; to leave the world a bit better, whether by a healthy child, a garden patch or a redeemed social condition; to know even one life has breathed easier because you have lived. This is to have succeeded.*
>
> —**Ralph Waldo Emerson**

Here is a great story to illustrate the true message of this chapter.

One day a fisherman was lying on a beautiful beach, with his fishing pole propped up in the sand and his solitary line cast out into the sparkling blue surf. He was enjoying the warmth of the afternoon sun and the prospect of catching a fish.

About that time, a businessman came walking down the beach, trying to relieve some of the stress of his workday. He noticed the fisherman sitting on the beach and decided to find out why this fisherman was fishing instead of working harder to make a living for himself and his family. "You aren't going to catch many fish that way," said the businessman to the fisherman. "You should be working rather than lying on the beach!"

The fisherman looked up at the businessman, smiled and replied, "And what will my reward be?" "Well, you can get bigger nets and catch more fish!" was the businessman's answer. "And then what will my reward be?" asked the fisherman, still smiling. The businessman replied, "You will make money and you'll be able to buy a boat, which will then result in larger catches of fish!" "And then what will my reward be?" asked the fisherman again. The businessman was beginning to get a little irritated with the fisherman's questions. "You can buy a bigger boat, and hire some people to work for you!" he said.

"And then what will my reward be?" repeated the fisherman. The businessman was getting angry. "Don't you understand? You can build up a fleet of fishing boats, sail all over the world, and let all your employees catch fish for you!" Once again the fisherman asked, "And then what will my reward be?" The businessman was red with rage and shouted at the fisherman, "Don't you understand that you can become so rich that you will never have to work for your living again! You can spend all the rest of your days sitting on this beach, looking at the sunset. You won't have a care in the world!"

The fisherman, still smiling, looked up and said, "And what do you think I'm doing right now?"

Habits of Heroes

The conditioned mind has been programmed to be a doer, work each day on being. What is something your heart really wants to do, but you've been putting it off. Be courageous and go do it!!!

The Heroes' **I am** statements. Please take a few minutes several times a day to say these.

1. I am being.
2. I am manifesting what my heart desires.
3. I am feeling good.

Go to TonyEdgell.com/book-videos and watch chapter 9 video.

Chapter 10

WHO ARE YOU?

Certain things catch your eye, but pursue only those that capture your heart.

—American Indian Proverb

To be yourself in a world that is constantly trying to make you something else is the greatest accomplishment.

—Ralph Waldo Emerson

I think the reward for conformity is that everyone likes you except yourself.

—Rita Mae Brown

The entire life of the personal ego is continually in the grip of wanting, i. e., an attempt to seek fulfillment of desires through things that change and vanish. But there can be no real fulfillment through the transient things.

—Meher Baba

If you want to reach a state of bliss, then go beyond your ego and the internal dialogue. Make a decision to relinquish the need to control, the need to be approved, and the need to judge. Those are the three things the ego is doing all the time. It's very important to be aware of them every time they come up.

—Deepak Chopra

If you want to find your true purpose in life, know this for certain: Your purpose will only be found in service to others, and in being connected to something far greater than your body/mind/ego.

—Wayne Dyer

*B*ooks, courses and people call what I refer to as the conditioned mind, the ego. Terms used for the Hero/heart is the higher self or true self. This means we are using something internal to guide us, not programming from the conditioned mind/ego. In this chapter we're going to explore what the conditioned mind or ego is telling us and what the Hero is telling us.

The conditioned mind/ego believes we are separate from other humans. The conditioned mind/ego's favorite word is I/ me, us and them. How does this affect me, how do I benefit, how much time out of my life will it take to help you, my family, my country? If I give money to the person in need, I will have less money for myself.

The Hero's favorite word is WE, a more collaborative way of living life. How may I serve you? I have compassion and kindness for you. We have different color skin, come from different parts of the world and do different things, but we are human beings. We can make this world a loving and peaceful world.

The conditioned mind/ego believes that making mistakes and taking risks is a bad thing and hates making mistakes. The next time you make a mistake, listen to the inner chatter of the conditioned mind/ego beating you up. Risk, the conditioned mind/ego's attitude is no thank you; I'm comfortable where I am.

The Hero knows we are not perfect and are never going to be, because that's the spice of life. It loves to laugh and make fun of its mistakes and never takes life seriously. It knows the only way to live its dreams is to do what society has defined as a risk.

The conditioned mind/ego believes we are what people think of us and how popular we are. How important is what people think of you? If reputation is very important, then we're not living our own life; we're living a life for other people and what pleases them. We love to focus on what we believe is important to us, like how many friends we have, if the friends are important people, how many people come to our parties, how many parties we're invited to, how many friends we have on Facebook, they might not like me if I say no, or what will they think of me if I don't do that.

The Hero loves people but doesn't allow the good opinions of people to hold them back from living their dreams. They understand that people are forming their opinions based on the conditioned mind/ego.

The conditioned mind/ego loves to complain. It will always tell you that this moment could be better if it were cooler, hotter, better weather, if I had more money, or if I had what my friends and neighbors have then I would be happy.

The Hero recognizes that this moment is perfect. I love and am grateful for my life.

The conditioned mind/ego loves to tell stories that stop us and then blame others. Can't is one of its favorite words. I can't do that because of (blank). I can't be like that, because this happened to me in the past so that's why I am like this.

The Hero in us knows it's powerful and was put on this planet for a purpose, to feel good, be alive and experience life.

The conditioned mind/ego is always in a hurry, fighting the clock. I'm running late, I need to do this and this before this time. I'm always so busy.

The Hero says slow down, stop and smell the roses and enjoy life.

The conditioned mind/ego believes it is anger, jealousy, fear, not worthy, revenge and shame.

The Hero knows it is love, joy, peace, kindness, compassion and well-being.

The conditioned mind loves to judge us, other people and pretty much everything.

The Hero only knows acceptance for one's self, everyone and life.

The conditioned mind wants to stay comfortable.

The Hero wants to live life to the fullest.

The conditioned mind believes everything external to us brings happiness and unhappiness.

The Hero knows joy is internal.

The conditioned mind listens to and believes in fear.

The Hero knows love and can live their dreams.

The conditioned mind believes that awards and honors define them as a person.

The Hero lives in the peaceful now and doesn't need approval from anyone.

The conditioned mind believes the programming.

The Hero listens to its courageous heart.

The conditioned mind believes in programming from society.

The Hero knows the truth of who it is.

The conditioned mind believes in being right.

The Hero knows that being light-hearted, having peace within, being relaxed and loose are key.

The conditioned mind is competition.

The Hero is cooperation.

The conditioned mind believes in scarcity.

The Hero knows abundance.

The conditioned mind believes in war.

The Hero knows peace.

The conditioned mind believes in what it's doing and worthiness is from doing.

The Hero knows who it's being.

The conditioned mind is trying to satisfy the programming that society told us would make us happy.

The Hero is manifesting what the heart desires.

The conditioned mind tries to do something.

The Hero knows it can manifest its heart's desires.

The conditioned mind believes we are defined by what we have. The house we live in, the car we drive, our appearance, our jewelry, etc., defines our worth as a person.

The Hero in us knows that what we have doesn't have anything to do with us. It enjoys and is grateful for material things but doesn't chase them believing they will bring happiness.

The conditioned mind thinks it's defined by the job we have and the position we hold. We've all been to cocktail parties where everyone is telling you who they are by what they do.

The Hero knows that what we do has nothing to do with who we are. It understands that what you're doing doesn't define who you are. A Hero does what makes their heart sing every day.

The conditioned mind wants to impress and prove its worth to people.

The Hero wants to improve who it's being in the world.

Awareness of the conditioned mind is extremely important to living as a Hero. We've had the ego for a long time so be patient with yourself and practice being aware without judgment.

If you believe in limitations, separations, judgment and fear of any kind, you have bought into the illusion that has been sold to you by the ego as reality. Likewise, if you respond to any person, place or thing with judgment, sadness, negativity, stress, anxiety, annoyance or anger, know that you have bought into the same illusion. These beliefs of what you are have been ingrained and reinforced in you in such a way that they have now become habitual. These habits, this habitual belief system (simply referred to as the ego-self or ego) is what you use to react to your daily experiences. This habitual belief system is mostly an unconscious belief system that manifests itself as your beliefs and attitudes. These beliefs and attitudes influence your daily reactions, responses and behaviors toward yourself, your fellow humans and the world in general. Like robots, any time you react with limitation, separation, judgment or fear, you are simply reacting as you have been programmed to. Eventually you will learn that this is not how you want to act, react, be or live. Slowly you will consciously become aware of your unconscious habitual belief system, and you will begin to de-program yourself. This should be a time of great celebration, for as you become aware of your programming you also begin to understand the possibility of choice. You learn that you indeed have the choice of seeing things as you've been programmed to, or reviewing what you currently believe to see if it fits with what you truly desire. You can now choose whether you want to continue with that limited belief system or replace it with a more empowering understanding. (James Blanchard Cisneros, *You Have Chosen to Remember: A Journey from Perception to Knowledge, Peace of Mind and Joy*, p. 4-5)

Habits of Heroes

Start paying attention to the programming, noise and chatter of the conditioned mind/ego. Don't judge or condemn it, just observe it with love and understanding.

The Heroes' **I am** statements. Please take a few minutes several times a day to say these.

1. I am accepting of myself and others.
2. I am living life to the fullest.
3. I am feeling good.

Go to TonyEdgell.com/book-videos and watch chapter 10 video.

Chapter 11

A THIEF IN THE NIGHT

There is something in every one of you that waits and listens for the sound of the genuine in yourself. It is the only true guide you will ever have. And if you cannot hear it, you will all of your life spend your days on the ends of strings that somebody else pulls.

—Howard Thurman

This is my simple religion. There is no need for temples; no need for complicated philosophy. Our own brain, our own heart is our temple; the philosophy is kindness.

—Dalai Lama

Whoever does not love does not know God, because God is love.

—1 John 4:8 (New International Version)

When you're too religious, you tend to point your finger to judge instead of extending your hand to help.

—Steve Maraboli

I believe in God, but not as one thing, not as an old man in the sky. I believe that what people call God is something in all of us. I believe that what Jesus and Mohammed and Buddha and all the rest said was right. It's just that the translations have gone wrong.

—John Lennon

The real question is not whether life exists after death. The real question is whether you are alive before death.

—Osho

I was raised in an extremely religious family. I had to go to church every Sunday morning and night, Wednesday evening and Friday night youth meetings. I remember driving to church Sunday morning and the whole family being angry with each other, because we were running late and my mother was forcing me and my brother to memorize the Bible verse that we had all week to work on and hadn't. Now we needed to have it memorized for Sunday school. I absolutely hated going to church.

I don't think there was anything that I hated more as a kid than going to church. Being at church never felt right to me; it seemed very unauthentic, or another way of saying it is that it didn't seem real and felt phony.

One of the scariest memories of my childhood was a movie that played at church about the rapture, *A Thief in the Night*. This movie was about what religious people call the rapture. Religious people believe that the rapture is when Jesus/God will call the believers or the good people to heaven. When this happens, all the religious believers will just vanish from the Earth. There could be a married people in bed at the same time and the believer will disappear into heaven and the nonbeliever will remain in bed without their spouse. There could be a believer driving a car and when the rapture takes place they'll vanish into heaven and the car will crash. The people that are nonbelievers that weren't taken by the rapture are left here on earth and it will be hell on Earth for them because of the violence, killing and anarchy in the world. That's why when I watched the movie, to say that it scared and frightened me is an understatement.

I was about eight years old, and my mind kept playing the scenes from the movie over and over in my head as I lay in bed with my eyes wide open, staring at the ceiling. After laying there for a long time, I went over to my parents' bedroom and woke them up because I was crying my eyes out. I told them that I didn't want to miss the rapture and have them disappear, leaving me in this scary world by myself. My mother said that I had to be saved, be a good boy and God would not punish me. I went back to my bedroom and stared at the ceiling again, telling myself that I'd be good, I could make myself like church and I wouldn't ever use those four letter words that God says are bad. I kept telling myself that I could do this, be a good boy and go to heaven. I wouldn't miss the rapture and go to that other place where you're burned alive forever.

Another memory I had as a child from church was a play on life after the rapture. The play had guys wearing masks, with real guns and they pretended to hold the church hostage because we were breaking the law. Churches were illegal after the rapture. They even took people outside and shot their guns off pretending to shoot them. I was programmed and conditioned to fear God growing up.

Growing up I was always very curious and had many questions about religion. When I asked religious people questions, the answer I always got was that I had to believe or they would get mad at me. These were the questions I had growing up: If God loved me, how could he put me in hell? Why do a lot of religious people seem negative and hateful? Why do religious people act differently on Sundays than they do the rest of the week? Why are certain words bad to say and other words that mean the same thing are OK to say? Why does the preacher know more about God than other people? Why are there so many different religions in the world? How do I know this is the right religion? Why is religion so complicated? What is the maximum number of sins I can commit before I go to hell? Are some sins worse than other sins? Are you judging people when you tell them they are going to hell? Why are some religious people so serious and don't enjoy life or have fun? What if someone lives in a Third World country, has never heard of God and dies, do they go to hell? What about someone that has murdered hundreds of people, gets saved and/

or finds God right before they die, do they go to heaven? Why do people get mad at me when I ask these questions?

Nobody could answer my questions. At about the age of 17, I decided I was an atheist. I never called myself an atheist, but in my heart I was. I couldn't believe what I had been taught to believe. Plus, I liked to drink alcohol, party, have sex and do things I was told were sins.

After 30 years of living as an undeclared atheist, fast forward to the present and something extremely bizarre happened to me; I found God or a higher power. I think a better term would be I experienced and do experience something every day that is bigger and greater than who I am. There are absolutely no words in this world to describe this experience. Through a Wayne Dyer video, *Inspiration-Your Ultimate Calling*, meditating and walking in nature, I've come to know this higher power that's inside of me, not outside. I will no longer refer to this higher power as God. The image I have of the word God is a man sitting on the throne watching us to see if we have been good or bad and I need to pray to him and ask for forgiveness for being bad and beg for things I want and for a better life. This higher power inside of me is the complete opposite of that. It is not fear, judgment, sin, good and bad people like I was programmed; it is unconditional love for me and everyone. We are here to enjoy and love life!

Over the last several years, I have studied and been a part of spiritual practices, but I never understood what spirituality meant. I can finally tell you what spirituality means to me. It's becoming aware and experiencing a higher power that's inside of us. The way to do this is to turn off or tune out our conditioned mind's thoughts and become aligned with this higher power inside of us by choosing loving, joyful, peaceful thoughts, higher thoughts, words and actions. We have free will to choose these thoughts, words and actions, or to choose not to. When we choose higher thoughts we become aligned with a higher power and we experience the Hero inside of us. To experience this higher power we must go to it; it's acknowledging our free will and waiting for us.

Jesus, Mohammed and Buddha and all the religions in the world that I know of say the same thing; we have something invisible in us that connects us to our creator/higher power. That higher power only knows unconditional love, joy, peace, perfect health and abundance, and each one of us has a little spark of that inside of us. So, who we truly are inside at our core is unconditional love, joy, peace, perfect health and abundance. Unconditional love does not judge, criticize, use fear or hate, it's our conditioned mind that tries to change and twist what unconditional love means. It is our conditioning that keeps us away from this higher power.

I can assure you that there's nothing that you want more in life than to connect with the higher power inside of you. It might sound boring or weird to you, but there is no greater feeling in the world. When you're connected, you will know what the Hero inside of you desires. And that's when life becomes awesome, fun, exciting and feels great. In the remainder of this book, we will gain a clearer understanding and how to get closer to this amazing feeling.

I wanted to end this chapter with excerpt from With Arms Wide Open by Creed. Due to copyright laws, I was unable to keep the words to the song in the book. Please do a search for the lyrics With

Arms Wide Open by Creed and read the last paragraph or verse as part of the journey to be a Hero.

There are no coincidences in the Universe. You were meant to read this chapter, this book. My wish for you is to have your arms wide open under the sunlight with tears of joy streaming down your face. The Hero inside will show you everything.

Habits of Heroes

Ask yourself, is what I'm about to do, say or think loving, kind, peaceful and compassionate.

The Heroes' **I am** statements. Please take a few minutes several times a day to say these.

1. I am connected to a higher power.
2. I am truth.
3. I am feeling good.

Go to TonyEdgell.com/book-videos and watch chapter 11 video.

Chapter 12

EXPERIENCE LIFE
ANEW WITH LOVE

The purpose of life is to live it, to taste experience to the utmost, to reach out eagerly and without fear for newer and richer experience.

—**Eleanor Roosevelt**

Freedom is the right to live as we wish.

—**Epictetus**

The real point of being alive is to evolve into the person you were meant to be.

—**Oprah Winfrey**

It matters not who you love, where you love, why you love, when you love or how you love, it matters only that you love.

—John Lennon

Love is not a mere sentiment. Love is the ultimate truth at the heart of creation.

—Rabindranath Tagore

When the power of love overcomes the love of power, the world will know peace.

—Jimi Hendrix

Every gun that is made, every warship launched, every rocket fired, signifies in the final sense a theft from those who hunger and are not fed, those who are cold and are not clothed.

—Dwight D. Eisenhower

I can't for the life of me imagine that God would say, "I will punish you because you are black. You should have been White. I will punish you because you are a woman; you should have been a man. I will punish you because you are homosexual. You ought to have been heterosexual." I can't for the life of me believe that is how God sees things.

—Archbishop Desmond Tutu

*I*t's time to challenge the conditioned mind again. You are a spiritual being having a temporary human experience, not a human being having a spiritual experience. What that means is that you have something inside of you that is invisible/observer/soul/higher self/universe/Hero/heart, it doesn't matter what we call it, and it came to experience life and it does this through our bodies. We experience life with our five senses and through duality. The way we're connected is through feelings. Feelings we sense when our conditioned mind is quiet, it's our guidance and our way of knowing. Emotions like anger, frustration, doubt, boredom, sadness, guilt, greed, impatience, unforgiving, jealousy, fear, envy, etc., come from programming and they allow the conditioned mind to control us.

The Hero/heart/soul that's in us is connected to the other side of the human experience. We were here before birth and when we leave this temporary body we will return. Yes, the thing you're in right now to experience life is made from the elements of Earth, it is temporary and will eventually die and decompose, but what's inside us is infinite and lives forever.

Earth, this place we call home, is filled with opposites or duality. As a human being, there is no way of experiencing things without knowing the opposites. We would not know what hot is without experiencing cold, up without down, tall without short, rich without poor, perfect health without sickness, or love without hate/fear. The place we came from and are going back to is a place of unconditional love, peace, joy, abundance and perfect health. There would be no way of knowing what these conditions are without experiencing the opposite. One of the reasons we came to this world is to experience the opposite/duality. Imagine being at a restaurant and the waiter asks if you want vanilla or chocolate ice cream. You've never had either flavor, but you ask the waiter to describe the flavors and you make a decision from his description. We have to experience the flavors of ice cream to know and understand. That's what life is; we need to experience things to understand them, to know if we want to continue to experience it or want to choose something else. You are reading this, and you have evolved to a point that you know you want to experience something different out of life. This is the Hero inside of you letting you know it wants to do and experience something different. Love, joy, kindness, abundance and peace, it's in all of us. When we recognize and connect to our divine self, we unlock our higher power.

In the rest of this chapter, we will be looking at the duality in different things in life. Don't allow yourself to classify things as good or bad, but rather something we experienced and understand, because of that experience and we're ready to evolve into something more empowering in life.

Duality of Love

I believe love is a very simple thing, but our conditioned mind can really twist this and make it confusing. Let's look at duality, the opposite or the dark side we've seen and experienced with love. The duality of love is not helping someone, because you're concerned what will happen to you or how you will be perceived. The duality of love is pointing your finger, judging, holding grudges, being ungrateful and criticizing someone. The duality of love is telling someone you're an authority and an expert in the rules of life and someone having sex with the same sex is wrong. The duality of love is telling someone they're going to hell. The duality of love is supporting or being a part of violence or killing other humans because you're government says it's legal and right.

Love

Love is seeing the hitchhiker who is dirty with old torn clothes and giving them a ride. Love is seeing the homeless person and caring for them like they were part of your family. Love is putting someone else's concerns ahead of yours and asking how you can be of service to them. Love is freedom for yourself and everyone in the world. Love is being in a state of gratitude, harmony and forgiveness. Love is having an understanding of people who live in other countries and knowing we are all one. Love is seeing the perfection and beauty in everyone. Love is strong and stands for all that is true and has no problem being the minority opinion. Love kisses the broken. Love hugs those that hurt. Love embraces the lonely. Love befriends the lost. Love is a kind word to everyone.

Duality of Peace

The duality of peace is yelling or flipping off another driver on the road. The duality of peace is thinking if other people and the world were different, we would be at peace and happy. The duality of peace believes violence and killing solves problems.

Peace

Peace is being in love with yourself, everyone and everything in this universe.

Duality of Joy

The duality of joy is doing what others tell you will make you happy. The duality of joy is caring what others think of you. The duality of joy is making decisions with the conditioned mind and thousands of years of peoples' programming telling you what's good or bad.

Joy

Joy is living and fulfilling your purpose in life. Joy is a byproduct of loving and being peaceful. Joy is the feeling of a romantic love, because you love someone unconditionally, without judgment or conditions.

Duality of Abundance

The duality of abundance is sickness, disease; not doing what makes your heart sing, not enjoying life every day, not being your true self and poverty. The duality of abundance is being afraid you don't have enough and not sharing your abundance.

Abundance

Abundance is perfect health, freedom to express our heart's desires, and having the resources to express our heart's desires, sharing, loving life and being true to who we are.

Duality of Compassion and Kindness

The duality of being compassionate and kind is being harmful, cruel or ignoring the need to help in the universe. When we do this, we are listening to the conditioned mind program instead of our heart.

Compassion and Kindness

Being compassionate and kind is listening to our hearts on how to treat everything in the universe, having empathy for everything in the universe and an understanding that we are all one.

One day at my old job, I heard two devout Catholics talking about how great church was the previous day. The very next day I overheard them talking about a man that used to be their boss and no longer worked there, and what he was doing now. They were saying how much they hated him and how happy they would be and how much better the world would be if he died. Another time I heard coworkers discussing that we should invade another country and kill everyone. Who do you choose to be in this world? What do you want to experience?

We are at an amazing point in history and evolution. We have experienced and seen duality and the opposite of what we want to experience. We are realizing that we can change what we want to experience in life by listening to our hearts and changing our programing. The more individuals choose to experience love, peace, joy, abundance, kindness, compassion and peace, the more there will be more love, peace, joy, abundance, kindness, compassion, and peace in the universe as a whole. There is no good or bad. We needed to experience darkness to know light. Now it's time for mankind to experience and evolve into the light of life. Love is not some sentimental thing to be embarrassed about; it can change your life and the world as we know it.

I'll end this chapter with quotes from my Hero, Martin Luther King, Jr., a man who taught us how to love our enemies and a man who changed the world with love. When his family's home was bombed, it never stopped him from working on equality for mankind, because he listened to his courageous heart. He was murdered for making the world a better place. In honor of you Martin Luther King, Jr., your message of love still holds true for us today.

Darkness cannot drive out darkness: only light can do that. Hate cannot drive out hate: only love can do that.

Our lives begin to end the day we become silent about things that matter.

If you can't fly then run, if you can't run then walk, if you can't walk then crawl, but whatever you do you have to keep moving forward.

I have decided to stick to love...Hate is too great a burden to bear.

Let no man pull you so low as to hate him.

Never, never be afraid to do what's right, especially if the well-being of a person or animal is at stake. Society's punishments are small compared to the wounds we inflict on our soul when we look the other way.

The ultimate measure of a man is not where he stands in moments of comfort and convenience, but where he stands at times of challenge and controversy.

Only in the darkness can you see the stars.

Everybody can be great...because anybody can serve. You don't have to have a college degree to serve. You don't have to make your subject and verb agree to serve. You only need a heart full of grace. A soul generated by love.

Never forget that everything Hitler did in Germany was legal.

We must live together as brothers or perish together as fools.

People fail to get along because they fear each other; they fear each other because they don't know each other; they don't know each other because they have not communicated with each other.

The choice is not between violence and nonviolence but between nonviolence and nonexistence.

A nation that continues year after year to spend more money on military defense than on programs of social uplift is approaching spiritual doom.

Love is the only force capable of transforming an enemy to a friend.

Life's most persistent and urgent question is, 'What are you doing for others?'

Hatred paralyzes life; love releases it. Hatred confuses life; love harmonizes it. Hatred darkens life; love illuminates it.

An individual has not started living until he can rise above the narrow confines of his individualistic concerns to the broader concerns of all humanity.

Our scientific power has outrun our spiritual power. We have guided missiles and misguided men.

Every man must decide whether he will walk in the light of creative altruism or in the darkness of destructive selfishness.

Returning violence for violence multiplies violence, adding deeper darkness to a night already devoid of stars... Hate cannot drive out hate: only love can do that.

The day we see the truth and cease to speak is the day we begin to die.

The first question which the priest and the Levite asked was: 'If I stop to help this man, what will happen to me?' But...the good Samaritan reversed the question: 'If I do not stop to help this man, what will happen to him?'

Now there is a final reason I think that Jesus says, "Love your enemies." It is this: that love has within it a redemptive power. And there is a power there that eventually transforms individuals. Just keep being friendly to that person. Just keep loving them, and they can't stand it too long. Oh, they react in many ways in the beginning. They react with guilt feelings, and sometimes they'll hate you a little more at that transition period, but just keep loving them. And by the power of your love they will break down under the load. That's love, you see. It is redemptive, and this is why Jesus says love. There's something about love that builds up and is creative. There is something about hate that tears down and is destructive. So love your enemies.

Habits of Heroes

Listen and feel the Hero inside of you that only knows love; it's very quiet and subtle, not loud and controlling like the conditioned mind. Ask yourself every evening, "Have I loved enough?"

The Heroes' **I am** statements. Please take a few minutes several times a day to say these.

1. I am love.
2. I am peace.
3. I am feeling good.

Go to TonyEdgell.com/book-videos and watch chapter 12 video.

Chapter 13

THE GREATEST LIE EVER TOLD

Self-worth and self-love is so key to making the best choices for ourselves, such a valuable lesson to learn. Love yourself and believe in yourself, don't wait for or depend upon anyone else to do it for you. Give yourself this precious gift.

—Bela Patel

If you ever struggle with self-worth, just know that it's coming from your old conditioned mind. The truth is that you're on a powerful path of transformation. As the old stories disappear, you know that you're a talented, beautiful, worthy person, a being of the universe. You are realizing

99

your greatness now, and you have everything you need to bring your dreams into fruition.

—**Lara Baeza Fernandez**

The greatest gift you will ever receive is the gift of loving and believing in yourself. Guard this gift with your life. It is the only thing that will ever truly be yours.

—**Tiffany Loren Rowe**

You have been criticizing yourself for years, and it hasn't worked. Try approving of yourself and see what happens.

—**Louise L. Hay**

To forgive is to set a prisoner free and discover that the prisoner was you.

—**Lewis B. Smedes**

You were born whole, complete and perfect. You were born beautifully unique. You are love and light. Allow yourself to be the true you. Let go of everything else that doesn't feel right to you, let go of all of the lies you have been told. Deep down, you really know the truth. Trust yourself. Love yourself.

—**Bela Patel**

*S*omewhere on our journey through life, someone (parents, teachers, uncles, brothers, sisters, coaches, etc.) might have told us that something was wrong with us and that we weren't perfect. Here are some of the things that might have been said as we were growing up: you are ugly, stupid, different from other kids, bad, a troublemaker, odd, lazy, not fun, weird, dumb, fat, shy, worthless, why can't you be more like your brother/sister? The craziest part about these things is that the conditioned mind believed all of this, and we've developed programs in us with this belief. This is the greatest lie ever told. The creator of the universe doesn't create anything but beauty and perfection. It's this lie, more than anything else that holds us back from living the life we were meant to live. We don't think we're worthy of living and realizing our dreams.

Imagine being born and growing up to adulthood on an island with no media at all, no TV, magazines, Internet, etc. The people on the island wouldn't know a standard of beauty created by the media on how beautiful they are. Everyone would be beautiful to us because we wouldn't have been programmed by the media; telling us who is and who is not beautiful. In today's society we are flooded with images of someone else's definition of what beauty is and what we need to do or wear to make us look great. People are dying from anorexia because their programming tells them they aren't thin and beautiful and they need to look a certain way to be beautiful. You are beautiful, inside and out, no matter what the media and programming have you believing.

Heroes know that love and peace are controlled from the inside. The more loving and at peace we are with ourselves, the more loving and peaceful we are with everyone around us. The more we dislike, hate and criticize ourselves, the more we dislike, hate and criticize the people around us. Love does not flow to you it flows from you, the more you give the more you have. It's a gift that can be made to grow only by giving it away. I wrote earlier in the book about pointing fingers and talking badly about people. The people that need to say bad things about other people do it because they don't feel good about themselves. They believe saying bad things about other people will make them feel better about themselves. People that are hurting hurt others. People that are healed, heal others.

I have something very important for you to do. It could be possibly the most important thing you've ever done; it's extremely simple, but the conditioned mind will probably fight you. Look at yourself in the mirror and repeat after me, "I am beautiful and I love who I am."

This might start a battle between the conditioned mind and the Hero inside. The conditioned mind could tell you how stupid this is and how it doesn't add any value to your life, but the Hero is gently telling you that it's time to heal. Ask yourself this question, why can't I do this? It's only me and the mirror there isn't anyone else to stop me or laugh. Who is that voice telling me how stupid this is and where is it coming from? You are courageous! You can do this. I believe in you!

Things that will help you connect to the Hero and your inner beauty:

Ask the higher power to help you become a more loving and peaceful person. Believe you will get help and become a loving and peaceful person.

Forgive yourself and everyone, even the people that told you the lies from the past that said you weren't good enough. We think by not forgiving someone it's hurting them, but it's really hurting us; let go of the poison that's disempowering you.

Laugh at yourself and life. Loosen up, life is about having fun and laughing not being serious and offended all of the time.

Share your time, money or both to help someone or something in the universe. Just look around and listen to the Hero inside you. The conditioned mind needs to tell people to take credit and be recognized, but the Hero inside of you does it because it feels right and doesn't need to tell anyone or be recognized.

Be patient. You have lived with the conditioned mind programming for a long time. Today's society has been conditioned for instant results, people pop pills to feel good right away and drive through fast food chains for instant gratification.

That story that the conditioned mind plays over and over telling you you're not good enough and not worthy is a bunch of BULL! Those are the thoughts of someone that doesn't feel good about themselves and said something bad about you to make them feel better. You have experienced the not being worthy and are ready to experience the duality of empowerment. You are an inspired, empowered and courageous Hero and you will fulfill the dreams that you desire. No good or bad, you're just ready to experience something new in your life.

The lyrics to Beautiful by Christina Aguilera and Perfect by Pink had been written below. Due to copyright laws, I was unable to keep the words to the song in the book. Please do a search for the lyrics to Beautiful by Christina Aguilera and Perfect by Pink and read them as part of the journey to be a Hero.

Habits of Heroes

Look into those beautiful eyes in the mirror and tell yourself you're beautiful and perfect. When you're doing this, if it feels right, play

Christina Aguilera's *Beautiful* and Pink's *Perfect*. There is no one in the world that can do this for you and no one will ever be able to convince you that you are beautiful and perfect until you know you are.

The Heroes' **I am** statements. Please take a few minutes several times a day to say these.

1. I love myself.
2. I am beautiful.
3. I am perfect.
4. I am feeling good.

Go to TonyEdgell.com/book-videos and watch chapter 13 video.

Chapter 14

THE END

Your weakness enables you to help others. It's the broken who become masters at mending. Your most effective ministry can come out of your most painful experiences. The things you're most reluctant to share are often the very things God will use to help others.

—The Word For You Today

Everyone's life is a warning or an example.

—Tony Robbins

The purpose of life is not to win. The purpose of life is to grow and to share. When you come to look back on all that you have done in life, you will get more satisfaction from the pleasure you have brought into other people's lives than you will from the time that you outdid and defeated them.

—Harold Kushner

There is no Them. There are only facets of us.

—John Green

Above all, be the Heroine of your life, not the victim.

—Nora Ephron

WHEN you call yourself an Indian or a Muslim or a Christian or a European, or anything else, you are being violent. Do you see why it is violent? Because you are separating yourself from the rest of mankind, when you separate yourself by belief, by nationality, by tradition, it breeds violence. So a man who is seeking to understand violence does not belong to any country, to any religion, to any political party or partial system; he is concerned with the total understanding of mankind.

—Jiddu Krishnamurti

*Y*es, I am a Hero! I did it! I wrote this book. I ignored the chatter of the conditioned mind. Thoughts like, who do I think I am writing a book, what am I going to say, I spell poorly and can barely write, how am I going to write a book, nobody's going to read it, who am I to write a spiritual book? But I ignored it and gave those negative thoughts no energy and turned to my higher, true, divine self. What you are now reading is possible because I made a choice to listen to my Hero. And the longer I wrote the easier it got until there was no chatter.

Imagine yourself as an elderly person in a nursing home with one week to live. When you look back on your life, what will cause you to be grateful and put a smile on your face? Or will you have regrets about the things you didn't do or say? What will be going through your mind? Will you be wishing you worked a few more hours? Spent more time with your children and grandchildren? Will you be proud of all the money you have in the bank? Will you be wishing you had more status and toys? Will you be proud of the position you held at work? Will you have regrets of not following your dream? Will you be wishing that you could talk about more people? Will you be proud of all the times when someone was wrong and you were right? Will it be the people you helped make their lives easier and better? Will it be all the love, kindness and compassion you've shown the world? Will it be things you did to make this universe more beautiful? Will you be saying, "Damn, that was awesome! I wish I could take that ride again."? Will you have regrets and wishing you could do it over? I have some really bad news; one day we're all leaving this world. What do you want your legacy to be?

There are two ways to live. We can choose to live from the conditioned mind, or we can choose to live from our heart and soul. Living from our conditioned mind is comfortable, because it's what we have been conditioned to think and do, what we have always done and how most people live their lives. When you live your life as a Hero, people will think that you are weird and different, because you won't have the thinking and consciousness of the majority. But you will be filled with joy for living the life you were meant to live.

The conditioned mind is thinking as a group, tribe or the majority. It's living unconsciously because it's living automatically from past conditioning and programming. Unconsciousness is where being right is the most important thing to us; my political party is right yours is wrong; the land I live in is right and the foreign land you live in is wrong; my race, nationality and gender is right yours is wrong; my group and tribe is right so I have a right to use violence and kill you, your group, tribe and family; I'm afraid that I don't have enough so I'll keep stockpiling, in a constant state of wanting and needing more never feeling satisfied; I have to impress my family, friends and neighbors with my material wealth; what will people think of me if I no longer live my life like them; if you don't follow the rules and are bad you'll go to hell; my rules and religion are right, yours are wrong; there are people that are above me and below me; I'm controlled by fear; I worship and envy other people and their lives; external things will make me happy.

The Hero's way of being and consciousness is love, peace, joy, compassion, service, kindness, harmony and freedom for everyone and everything in the world.

Grab your TV remote and scroll through the channels for an hour or two; you are viewing worldwide unconsciousness— the beliefs from the tribe, group thinking, and conditioned mind's thoughts. There's no denying this. What is on TV for our viewing pleasure is really how the majority of mankind thinks and believes.

The conditioned mind (unconsciousness) is from thousands of years of being conditioned and with that comes strong emotions and brain chatter. The brain chatter and emotions consist of all the negative and fearful programming that keeps us in automatic mode. These are thoughts and emotions that we are comfortable with. To become a Hero we can't let emotions and chatter stop us. We need turn off the chatter and listen to our heart. When we have no attachment to emotions and chatter, we're in alignment with a higher power.

There is no right or wrong, there are choices and experiences. What do you want your experience to be? Do you want to experience the status quo of unconsciousness or feeling alive like a Hero? Your last week of being in the physical form, which one will put a grateful smile on your face?

Your life is your message to the world. Make it inspiring.
—**Lorrin L. Lee**

You may say I'm a dreamer, but I'm not the only one. I hope someday you'll join us. And the world will live as one.
—**John Lennon**

Habits of Heroes

Observe your conditioned mind's thoughts, but don't judge them because they are not you. The conditioned mind cannot survive without thoughts from the past and future, live in the now.

The Heroes' **I am** statements. Please take a few minutes several times a day to say these.

1. I am divine consciousness.
2. I am service.
3. I am feeling good

Go to TonyEdgell.com/book-videos and watch chapter 14 video.

Chapter 15

I AM THE CREATOR
OF MY LIFE

I learned that the real creator was my inner self. That desire to do something is God inside talking through us.

—**Michele Shea**

Create the highest, grandest vision possible for your life, because you become what you believe.

—**Oprah Winfrey**

The intuitive mind is a sacred gift and the rational mind is a faithful servant. We have created a society that honors the servant and has forgotten the gift.

—**Albert Einstein**

111

Once you become consciously aware of just how powerful your thoughts are, you will realize everything in your life is exactly how you allow it to be.

—Melanie Moushigian Koulouris

You are a living magnet. What you attract into your life is in harmony with your dominant thoughts.

—Brian Tracy

He who controls his own thoughts, controls his own destiny.

—Ross Arntson

A man is but the product of his thoughts. What he thinks, he becomes.

—Mahatma Gandhi

You must learn a new way to think before a new way to be.

—Marianne Williamson

*W*ords cannot express how inspired I feel writing this chapter. It has been a long and challenging journey to find the information in this chapter. It has become crystal clear to me why I took this journey; so I could share, teach and give this information to others. I am extremely grateful for how creating this book has allowed me to serve. This chapter can change your life forever. You will learn how to experience a life of joy and passion, and how to manifest your heart's desires and become the person you were meant to be, how to be a Hero.

Everyone has a beautiful gift they want to share with the world which is our heart's desires. The key to manifesting this gift is nonattachment to thoughts from the conditioned mind. When we don't attach to our thoughts, we find the perfection inside of us, our Hero who's aligned with our dreams. This is what you have been searching for, go to it and your life will never be the same. Go to it!

> *Our knowledge has made us cynical; our cleverness, hard and unkind. We think too much and feel too little. More than machinery, we need humanity. More than cleverness, we need kindness and gentleness.*
> —**Charlie Chaplin,** in 'The Great Dictator'

The world and universe we live in operates with feelings, frequencies and vibrations, which are completely different than what we've been taught. We've been taught 1+1=2. I'm not telling you that 1+1 doesn't equal 2, but what I will tell you is that we have been taught to use our intellect and not our feelings and guidance from the Hero/heart. Someone connected to their Hero and higher power uses their feelings as a guide and their intellect as a tool. As human beings, using and relying upon the conditioned mind, we have lost the concept of listening to our feelings. We are like robots running around making decisions with the conditioned mind as our guide.

When I visited New York City and rode the subway, it was a fascinating experience for me. Nobody made eye contact or talked to anyone. I actually tried to make small talk with someone and I wasn't very successful and it became very awkward for both of us. This is what life looks like when we use the conditioned mind instead of our hearts. The people on the subway aren't good or bad, they're just experiencing the opposite of being a feeling person. This is one of the experiences in my life that made me realize I needed to share with others that there is a different way of living and experiencing life.

Being a feeling person gives you the sensation that your chest is wide open and you feel love, compassion and kindness for everyone and everything. The opposite of this is our chest feels closed and we're thinking with the conditioned mind of the things in the past and future.

The universe we live in operates with the frequency of energy or how fast energy is vibrating. Everything we feel, see, touch, smell and hear is energy at a different frequency. I know it sounds crazy and hard to believe, but this is something science has proven. I'm looking at a chair and it's very hard for my conditioned mind to grasp this because it only uses its five senses to draw conclusions and make decisions.

If everything in the universe is vibrating energy, and we're in the universe—that means we are vibrating energy. And our vibration is who we are internally. Right now our whole being is at a certain energy vibration and our thoughts and words are at certain energy vibrations. Every thought and word we have is a different energy vibration, depending on what we say or think. How we feel is how we're vibrating; the better we feel, the higher our vibration. The higher our vibration, the more aligned we are with our heart's desires. How do you feel? Do you feel joyful, angry, loving, not worthy? How do you feel about living your dreams and doing what your heart desires? How do you feel about living a life with passion? When you wake up in the morning do you feel playful, alive and joyful for the day ahead?

To manifest our heart desire is be, do and have in that exact order. This is completely different from what we've been taught. We've been taught to do and keep doing with lots of effort, stress, time, no joy, pain and sweat, and eventually we will get what we want, but the universe doesn't work that way. What happens is we get more frustrated, do more and try more; the more we do this, the farther away we get from being a person that feels good and recognizes our heart's desires. Only changing thoughts will manifest our heart's desires easily and effortlessly. As I said earlier, we attract everything into our lives by being, then doing, and then having. Please write this down and hang it where you see it all the time as a daily reminder.

Being → Doing → Having

Some of the personal development courses I attended talked about growing as a person and how I would have what I wanted in life. I thought that meant the more information I knew, the more it would help me grow. So I studied a lot of information and my conditioned mind grew but my Hero never did. I was not living from my heart. I was doing before I changed my being. To live our dreams and heart's desires, we need to raise our energy vibration and change who we're being or who our programming believes we are. Then we know what our hearts desires and why our spirit came to Earth; to be full of life and joy, it's unnatural not to be joyful.

Wisdom to Change Your Energy and Vibration

Nothing changes until you change; everything changes once you change.

—**Unknown**

There is nothing outside of us that can make us happy, mad, sad, upset, miserable or secure. It's the conditioned mind that tells us how to react when that certain thing happens or that person does something that makes us mad and when I do that or have that I'll be finally happy. Be extremely thankful with the life you have right now and grateful for everything you have, the bed you sleep in, food, water, shelter, family and friends, etc. The conditioned mind is unappreciative and believes life could be much better; the spirit inside of you is grateful for everything.

The cave you fear to enter holds the treasure you seek.

—**Joseph Campbell**

The comfort zone is an enemy and it tries to hold us back from living our dreams. What is the comfort zone? It's everything the conditioned mind has been programmed to do or say, regardless if it makes us feel good or not. It's in the programming so it's comfortable and we continue to do it. If we learn as a kid that we have to work hard and stay busy to be worthy and good as an adult, we will stay busy and work hard even if it doesn't make us happy. Or maybe we rebelled from that teaching and our programming is unmotivated—our programming is *comfortable* being unmotivated. People go to jobs they don't like for 30 years, but they're comfortable doing it. I heard a story about how baby elephants are tied to a post at circuses and when they're adults they no longer have to be tied to the post and they never leave, they're comfortable and programmed to stay there. When we're uncomfortable or thinking about being uncomfortable, the conditioned mind produces the biggest enemy to being a Hero— fear. To live as a Hero, you will need to do things that make you uncomfortable and fearful.

The conditioned mind has low energy thoughts. These thoughts are not who we are deep down. The conditioned mind loves to tell us how bad people and things are and how right we are. You are not your thoughts; they come from past conditioning, so don't attach to them. And the way to do that is through meditation. Meditation will bring you in harmony with the universe which operates with love, joy, harmony and peace.

What do you desire? The conditioned mind has a very hard time with this question. It might not have the answer or it might have a list of 20 things that are centered on what someone else told us would make us happy. When we stop paying attention to, or turn off the thoughts from our conditioned mind, we find our heart's desires and this is when life gets juicy. Our heart knows what we desire and when we do it, our heart's desire serves the planet, brings a great lifestyle, we're inspired to do it and our life's journey makes sense—has meaning.

The reason you want every single thing that you want, is because you think that you will feel really good when you get there. But, if you don't feel good on your way to there, you can't get there. You have to be satisfied with what-is while you're reaching for more.

—**Abraham-Hicks, Jerry & Esther Hicks**

We have an internal meter to let us know if we're allowing our heart's desires to manifest. Feeling badly and having negative emotions indicates a resistance to our heart's desires. Feeling great and having positive feelings is an indicator of allowing ourselves to manifest our heart's desires. If we are thinking and talking about people that are poor and starving, corrupt Wall Street, bad politicians and government, war, our boss, violence, negative news and anything else that impacts negatively on how we're feeling, we feel badly, and we are not attracting our heart's desires. Nobody but you is responsible for the way you feel. The best thing we can do for this world is to raise our energy vibration and live with passion. Then we will have a better appreciation for life and have a greater desire to serve humanity and this beautiful planet.

I am! These are two powerful words that tell the universe what we want to experience in life. When we say I am broke, always late, stressed, mad, worthless, or if you add the word "not" before I am not loved, I am not healthy, I am not smart, I am not good enough, I am not fun enough, we send that energy out to the universe. Become aware of and stop using I am to create something you don't want and use it as a tool to create what you do want, like each of the I am statements after each chapter.

Focus on thoughts, words and feelings of what you want. What you don't want is a tool; you take the negative and make it a positive of what you want. You are in a huge smorgasbord called life. Focus on everything you want and ignore everything you don't want.

Co-creation with your Hero is a desire, but a want and need has something to do with fear, materialism and competition about having more or being better than someone else, desperation, dissatisfaction and the belief that if-we-get-this, it will make us happy. It's needy and can never be satisfied. A desire is from a higher power, it's bigger than us, it comes from love and we come alive with passion.

Another form of a wanting is attachment. Attachment is based on the fear that our desire will not manifest and we need it to be safe, secure and happy. Go by your feelings. Are you stressed, feeling tense, in a bad mood or not feeling like yourself when you think or work on your desires? This is a sign that we have attachment. When creating with nonattachment we're committed, excited and feeling great. When meditating, go inward and ask, "Is my desire for the highest good for myself and all of life?"

There is a nonphysical world out there that our conditioned mind cannot identify with, because it only knows and trusts its five senses. When our thoughts are loving, joyful, peaceful, kind and inspirational, we have the invisible life force/God force flowing through us, helping and guiding us with our desires.

Trust and believe that you will manifest your desires and leave the how to a higher power.

> *The world of spirit is the source of all power. There never was and never will be any other source of power. What the world calls power is really fear that leads to manipulation and control of others, which in turn leads to violence and suffering. Real power is:*
> *the power to create,*
> *the power to transform,*
> *the power to love,*
> *the power to heal, and*
> *... the power to be free.*
> *Real power comes from our connection to our deepest self, to what is real.*
>
> **—Dr. Deepak Chopra**

The way to manifest your heart's desires is to be unattached to thoughts, change your being and raise your vibration. In the rest of this chapter, I will be giving you a guide on how to become unattached to thoughts, change who you're being and raise your vibration. Some or all of these could make you uncomfortable, because they might not have been taught or programmed when growing up. You can either be comfortable or live your dreams. I promise you, deep down inside you are more powerful than you could ever imagine. To be successful with the program you must be gentle with yourself. The spirit inside of you wants to do this and experience something new in life.

The 90 Day Program:
Change Your Being and Raise Your Energy

Motivation comes from others Inspiration comes from within.

—**Tim Porter**

Please commit to doing this for 90 days and see how you feel afterward. You might start feeling different after a few weeks or it could take longer. We have been programmed for quick and easy results, please be patient with the program and yourself.

The richest person is the one who is contented with what he has.

—**Robert C. Savage**

Take 10 to 15 minutes every day to say the things that you're grateful for and say them out loud and feel them. You can even have a journal where you write down two or three new things that you are grateful for every day. This is a huge step in overriding the conditioned mind and listening to your heart. There will be days when you don't feel like doing this; that's programming and emotions from the conditioned mind. Show the conditioned mind that you're in charge. Gratitude is a state of being.

Meditate 6 or 7 days a week, 20 minutes or more in the morning, and if you can't do it in the morning, do it at another time. Sit quietly in a comfortable, dimly lit spot with no distractions, relax and listen to your breathing. Please don't get frustrated if your thoughts distract you, this process will bring awareness to thoughts from the conditioned mind;

simply pretend your thoughts belong to someone else. Like anything else, with practice you will get a lot better, and eventually this will be a very rewarding experience. There are CDs and DVDs on meditation that you can purchase. There is no better way to get in touch with your heart and let go of your thoughts. Your thoughts are clouds and you are the sky watching the clouds.

> *A lot of people are afraid to say what they want. That's why they don't get what they want.*
>
> —**Madonna**

When you wake up in the morning start taking control and say yes to your life, everything in it and how perfect your life is. In the morning, before or after your meditation, or maybe on your way to work, get really excited about your life. Say with excitement and out loud for 5 or 10 minutes a day, I love my life, I love myself, I'm excited about my life, I'm living my dreams and I'm manifesting my heart's desires. How do you think you will be vibrating and feeling when you manifest your heart's desire? What you are doing through the process described is changing your energy vibration to a higher vibration. If you can't get excited about your life how are you going to manifest your desires and dreams? You are worthy to do this because you are a powerful creator.

> *It is very simple to be happy, but it is very difficult to be simple.*
>
> —**Rabindranath Tagore**

Drastically slow your life down. You know what needs to change to slow down. It's very hard if not impossible to get aligned with your Hero in a hectic fast-paced life. People take vacations to be relaxed and feel good; you can feel like that all the time. Be relaxed every day. The more relaxed you are, the closer you are to your heart. Get out into nature and open your heart to it; it can heal you. Just enjoy being.

> *Become more and more innocent, less knowledgeable and more childlike. Take life as fun - because that's precisely what it is!*
>
> **—Osho**

Stop taking life so seriously!!!!! Every day share lots of joyful belly laughs and loosen up. Watch children play and learn they live in the now because they have not be burdened with all these crazy, serious thoughts. Adults have forgotten how to play. Children can teach us a lot more than we could ever teach them. The meaning of life is to enjoy it, have fun and bring inspiration, love and beauty to the world. We have forgotten this. If you aren't thinking that way, you must delete that file.

Give up TV or almost all TV. Be very selective about what you allow in. You're in charge of your life. The TV is feeding your conditioned mind without you realizing it. Make sure that all the media you allow in is inspiring and empowering. Media that has low vibrations of violence, making someone or something wrong and sarcastic humor that makes another person look and feel badly is not going to get you closer to the life you were meant to live. Taking control is extremely empowering to know you are in control of your life and not the programming from society. How important is it to experience a joyful life?

When you are going through your day, look at people in the eyes, give them a beautiful smile and greet them. Their response or lack of response has nothing to do with you; it's about them. Be a Hero and spread your love and light in the world. When people ask you how you're doing, give them an inspiring high vibrational response like: I love my life, amazing, awesome, not a low energy response like: okay, good, all right. Give everyone hugs, a heartfelt hug filled with love, not the "pat your partner on the back like they have a contagious disease". Throughout the day, give appreciation and compliments to everyone. Start meeting and talking to strangers; get out of your comfort zone.

Changing food and fuel for the body was one of my biggest challenges. Nutrition is very important when it comes to your body; we know how horrible we feel after eating low energy foods. It's much easier to get in touch with your heart when your body feels great. This is very empowering, because you realize you're more powerful than the programing you received from thousands of hours of food commercials telling you what you should eat no matter what it does to your bodies or how it makes you feel. Six days a week eat only fruit, vegetables, nuts and lean protein, like fish, poultry or beef. On the seventh day eat whatever you want. Make delicious blended smoothies with fruits, coconut oil and vegetables and add some powdered protein. Make a great salad with a protein, and use olive oil as the dressing. Try eating only organic foods. Experiment with different ways of eating non-processed foods, vegetarian, vegan, paleo, blood type, raw and maybe a mixture of all of them. What makes you feel great? Another extremely important thing is to drink lots of water; if you're drinking city water, I highly recommend using a filtering system or buying water from the store. If you have a well, make sure to have the water tested regularly.

Alcohol, drugs, coffee, caffeine and energy drinks should not be consumed during this 90 day commitment. These are all things that are harming your divine body and keeping you at a low vibration. I promise you, in 90 days you will be feeling awesome and you won't need caffeine for energy, alcohol or drugs to feel good.

Exercise at least 30 minutes a day, six days a week. Do something that gets you moving and raises your heart rate, like lifting weights, hiking, riding a bike, yoga, aerobics classes, etc. Our spirits are taking a ride in a vehicle called a body; exercise makes the vehicle healthy and when we're healthy we feel good; and when we feel good we vibrate high energy.

I wrote earlier in the book about looking in the mirror and telling yourself how much you love yourself, how perfect and beautiful you are. Everywhere you go you take yourself with you, so it's important that you have a loving great relationship and be content with yourself for joy and freedom. Everyday look in the mirror for a few minutes a couple times a day at your best friend and say all the above and anything else you need to hear to be in love with you. This one of the greatest things you can do for yourself, humanity and the Universe. Do you control your thoughts or do your thoughts control you?

Energy is the essence of life. Every day you decide how you're going to use it by knowing what you want and what it takes to reach that goal, and by maintaining focus.

—Oprah Winfrey

Have a conversation with an imaginary person six or seven days a week on how you want your life to look in the future. Talk in the past tense as if your desire has already happened. Setting the stage of how we see our life as if it has already taken place. Add lots of juicy descriptive adjectives have lots of fun doing it and have the conversation out loud. Get really excited when talking and have your body vibrate and feel what that's like. Have a conversation with an imaginary person or a real one who will just listen and not question what you want. If you use a real person, choose that person carefully, because you don't want to bring in any low vibrational energy to your dreams.

The greatest thing will take place while you are on this journey; you'll figure out what your heart really desires. Don't stress by trying to make this happen, just relax and have fun. Just know the universe is perfect and this will happen at the perfect time. When you discover what your heart truly desires, add this into your conversation with your imaginary person. Make sure that your conversation is in the past tense, as if it already happened, and focus on what you want, not what you don't want.

The big question is how long until we are aligned with what our heart desires? The factors that come into this are how much of a desire do you have to experience alignment with your heart and living your dreams? How much desire do you have? A weaker desire will take longer, and stronger desire will take less time. How committed and excited are you to changing your vibration? The more committed you are, the less time it will take. How excited are you about this chapter and when you do the work to change your vibration? Other than that, it's up to this perfect universe which is called divine time. I will tell you this it is well worth it.

You have a huge choice to make. Do you close this book and never think about this again or push through your fears and comfort zone, and live the life you were meant to live? You are not the victim; you're the creator.

Your mission: be so busy loving your life you have no time for hate, regret or fear.

—**Karen Salmansohn**

Man has lost one quality, the quality of zestfulness. And without zest, what is life? Just waiting for death?
It can't be anything else. Only with zest do you live; otherwise you vegetate.

—**Osho**

What others deem as safe and predictable is often what leads one closer to being stale, boring and dead.

—**Jafree Ozwald**

Some people want it to happen, some wish it would happen, others make it happen.

—**Michael Jordan**

Everybody wants to grow but nobody wants to change.
—**Tony Robbins**

Habits of Heroes

Do the 90 day program.

The Heroes' **I am** statements. Please take a few minutes several times a day to say these.

1. I am a creator of my life.
2. I am aware of who I'm being, thoughts and words.
3. I am feeling great.

Go to TonyEdgell.com/book-videos and watch chapter 15 video.

Chapter 16

I Believe In You

All your dreams can come true if you have the courage to pursue them.

—Walt Disney

I searched for God and found only myself. I searched for myself and found only God.

—Sufi Proverb

You have brains in your head. You have feet in your shoes. You can steer yourself any direction you choose. You're on your own. And you know what you know. And YOU are the one who'll decide where to go...

—Dr. Seuss

There are two basic motivating forces: fear and love. When we are afraid, we pull back from life. When we are in love, we open to all that life has to offer with passion, excitement and acceptance. We need to learn to love ourselves first, in all our glory and our imperfections. If we cannot love ourselves, we cannot fully open to our ability to love others, or our potential to create. Evolution and all hopes for a better world rest in the fearlessness and open-hearted vision of people who embrace life.

—John Lennon

No one saves us but ourselves. No one can and no one may. We ourselves must walk the path.

—Buddha

The difference between what we do and what we are capable of doing would suffice to solve most of the world's problem.

—Mahatma Gandhi

For all things and non-things that you may ever want, understand that sometimes the fastest way to get them is to forget them, and to focus instead on just being the most amazing human being you can be. At which point all of your heart's desires, spoken or unspoken, will be drawn to you more powerfully than a magnet is drawn to steel.

—TUT… A Note from the Universe

People are often unreasonable, irrational, and self-centered. Forgive them anyway. If you are kind, people may accuse you of selfish, ulterior motives. Be kind anyway. If you are successful, you will win some unfaithful friends and some genuine enemies. Succeed anyway. If you are honest and sincere people may deceive you. Be honest and sincere anyway. What you spend years creating, others could destroy overnight. Create anyway. If you find serenity and happiness, some may be jealous. Be happy anyway. The good you do today, will often be forgotten. Do good anyway. Give the best you have, and it will never be enough. Give your best anyway.

—**Mother Teresa**

Here's to the crazy ones. The misfits. The rebels. The trouble-makers. The round heads in the square holes. The ones who see things differently. They're not fond of rules. And they have no respect for the status-quo. You can quote them. Disagree with them. Glorify, or vilify them. But the only thing you can't do is ignore them. Because they change things. They push the human race forward. And while some may see them as the crazy ones, we see genius. Because the people who are crazy enough to think they can change the world Are the ones who do.

—**Steve Jobs**

Our deepest fear is not that we are inadequate. Our deepest fear is that we are powerful beyond measure. It is our light, not our darkness that most frightens us. We ask ourselves, Who am I to be brilliant, gorgeous, talented, fabulous.

Actually, who are you not to be? You are a child of God. Your playing small does not serve the world. There is nothing enlightened about shrinking so that other people won't feel insecure around you. We are all meant to shine, as children do. We were born to make manifest the glory of God that is within us. It's not just in some of us; it's in everyone. And as we let our own light shine, we unconsciously give other people permission to do the same. As we are liberated from our own fear, our presence automatically liberates others.

—**Marianne Williamson**

I believe in you. Why do I believe in you? Because I know there's a Hero inside of you. All you need is courage to be the person who does the opposite of the majority and detaches from the conditioned mind to be aligned with your higher self. The reward for listening to your Hero is living your purpose in life; being empowered and alive, inspired, passionate and joyful for life, full of abundance; being a co-creator with the Universe and manifesting your heart's desires, loving life, going with the flow of life, living effortlessly and with ease and live the life you were meant to live. I BELIEVE IN YOU!

The lyrics to Hero by Mariah Carey had been written below. Due to copyright laws, I was unable to keep the words to the song in the book. Please do a search for the lyrics to Hero by Mariah Carey and read them as part of the journey to be a Hero.

Habits of Heroes

Believe in yourself and know that you are a Hero.

The Heroes' **I am** statements. Please take a few minutes several times a day to say these.

1. I am a Hero.
2. I am living my purpose.
3. I am feeling great.

Go to TonyEdgell.com/book-videos and watch chapter 16 video.

Chapter 17

WHAT ABOUT NOW?

How wonderful it is that nobody need wait a single moment before starting to improve the world.

—Anne Frank

I PROMISE MYSELF
To be so strong that nothing can disturb my peace of mind.
To talk health, happiness and prosperity to every person I meet.
To make all my friends feel that there is something worthwhile in them.
To look at the sunny side of everything and make my optimism come true.
To think only of the best and to expect only the best.

To be just as enthusiastic about the success of others as I am about my own.

To forget the mistakes of the past and to press on to the achievements of the future.

To wear a cheerful expression at all times and to give a smile to every living creature I meet.

To give so much time to improving myself that I have no time to criticize others.

To be too large for worry, too noble for anger, too strong for fear and too happy to permit the presence of trouble.

To think well of myself and to proclaim this fact to the world, not in loud words but in great deeds.

To live in the faith that the whole world is on my side, so long as I am true to the best that is in me.

—**The Secret** (the real power within me)

People talk about wishing, wanting and making the world better, but the only control we have on making the world more beautiful is the person staring at you in the mirror. Do you want to live in a world that's more beautiful? Then look in the mirror and point a finger at your beautiful self. It's easy to point the finger outward and say what's wrong and needs changing. It's much harder to point toward ourselves. You have a gift inside of you that the world needs; this gift is unique to you and only you can serve the world with it. The way to this gift is shedding the layers of conditioning and be happy and content in your own skin just being you. Fall in love with the person that goes everywhere with you—YOU! You are so much bigger than the stories you tell and the stories you have been told. The time to be you is now! The time to share your gift is now! The world needs your gift now! The time to be a Hero is now! The following excerpt captures the journey of a Hero.

A time comes in your life when you finally get...when, in the midst of all your fears and insanity, you stop dead in your tracks and somewhere the voice inside your head cries out...ENOUGH! Enough fighting and crying and blaming and struggling to hold on. Then, like a child quieting down after a tantrum, you blink back your tears and begin to look at the world through new eyes.

This is your awakening.

You realize it's time to stop hoping and waiting for something to change, or for happiness, safety and security to magically appear over the next horizon.

You realize that in the real world there aren't always fairy tale endings, and that any guarantee of "happily ever after" must begin with you...and in the process a sense of serenity is born of acceptance.

You awaken to the fact that you are not perfect and that not everyone will always love, appreciate or approve of who or what you are...and that's OK. They are entitled to their own views and opinions.

You learn the importance of loving and championing yourself...and in the process a sense of new found confidence is born of self-approval.

Your stop complaining and blaming other people for the things they did to you – or didn't do for you – and you learn that the only thing you can really count on is the unexpected.

You learn that people don't always say what they mean or mean what they say and that not everyone will always be there for you and everything isn't always about you.

So, you learn to stand on your own and to take care of yourself...and in the process a sense of safety and security is born of self-reliance.

You stop judging and pointing fingers and you begin to accept people as they are and to overlook their shortcomings and human frailties...and in the process a sense of peace and contentment is born of forgiveness.

You learn to open up to new worlds and different points of view. You begin reassessing and redefining who you are and what you really stand for.

You learn the difference between wanting and needing and you begin to discard the doctrines and values you've outgrown, or should never have bought into to begin with.

You learn that there is power and glory in creating and contributing and you stop maneuvering through life merely as a "consumer" looking for you next fix.

You learn that principles such as honesty and integrity are not the outdated ideals of a bygone era, but the mortar that holds together the foundation upon which you must build a life.

You learn that you don't know everything, it's not your job to save the world and that you can't teach a pig to sing. You learn the only cross to bear is the one you choose to carry and that martyrs get burned at the stake.

Then you learn about love. You learn to look at relationships as they really are and not as you would have them be. You learn that alone does not mean lonely.

You stop trying to control people, situations and outcomes. You learn to distinguish between guilt and responsibility and the importance of setting boundaries and learning to say NO.

You also stop working so hard at putting your feelings aside, smoothing things over and ignoring your needs.

You learn that your body really is your temple. You begin to care for it and treat it with respect. You begin to eat a balanced diet, drinking more water, and take more time to exercise.

You learn that being tired fuels doubt, fear, and uncertainty and so you take more time to rest. And, just food fuels the body, laughter fuels our soul. So you take more time to laugh and to play.

You learn that, for the most part, you get in life what you deserve, and that much of life truly is a self-fulfilling prophecy.

You learn that anything worth achieving is worth working for and that wishing for something to happen is different than working toward making it happen.

More importantly, you learn that in order to achieve success you need direction, discipline and perseverance. You learn that no one can do it all alone, and that it's OK to risk asking for help.

You learn the only thing you must truly fear is fear itself. You learn to step right into and through your fears because you know that whatever happens you can handle it and to give in to fear is to give away the right to live life on your own terms.

You learn to fight for your life and not to squander it living under a cloud of impending doom.

You learn that life isn't always fair, you don't always get what you think you deserve and that sometimes bad things happen to unsuspecting, good people…and you lean not to always take it personally.

You learn that nobody's punishing you and everything isn't always somebody's fault. It's just life happening. You learn to admit when you are wrong and to build bridges instead of walls.

You lean that negative feelings such as anger, envy and resentment must be understood and redirected or they will suffocate the life out of you and poison the universe that surrounds you.

You learn to be thankful and to take comfort in many of the simple things we take for granted, things that millions of people upon the earth can only dream about: a full refrigerator, clean running water, a soft warm bed, a long hot shower.

Then, you begin to take responsibility for yourself by yourself and you make yourself a promise to never betray yourself and to never, ever settle for less than you heart's desire.

You make it a point to keep smiling, to keep trusting, and to stay open to every wonderful possibility.

You hang a wind chime outside your window so you can listen to the wind.

Finally, with courage in your heart, you take a stand, you take a deep breath, and you begin to design the life you want to live as best as you can. (author unknown)

You ARE a Hero.

These are your **I am** statements. Live them every day.

1. I am self acceptance.
2. I love sharing my gift.
3. I am feeling good.

Go to TonyEdgell.com/book-videos and watch chapter 17 video.

Visit TonyEdgell.com to receive 5 free videos to find purpose, power, and the Hero you were meant to be.

9 781630 470593